NO DOGS IN CHINA

In 1949 the bamboo curtain clattered down over one-fifth of the people of the world. In one sudden twist of history, a vast community that had been militarily and politically allied with the West was transmuted into the ideological foe of everything the free world stands for. With the surprise intervention by Red China in Korea, a new alignment of world powers was confirmed and the bamboo curtain had been fastened down securely.

If the people of China were inadequately known in the years before the Red Revolution, all free intercourse between East and West was now interrupted completely. Chinese life could be described only by released westerners who had viewed it through prison bars, or it had to be interpreted from the incredibly distorted releases of the communist propaganda bureaus.

Suddenly, in 1956, China offered to open its doors to western reporters wishing to come and see what was really happening in their country. In the spring of 1957, William Kinmond, Staff Reporter for the Toronto Globe and Mail, entered Red China with assurances that he might travel where he wished and report what he liked—or disliked. This is his report on China at this moment in history.

WILLIAM KINMOND, a Canadian journalist, was a staff reporter for the highly respected Toronto Globe and Mail.

No Dogs in China

in China

A REPORT

ON CHINA

TODAY

WILLIAM

University of Toronto Press

KINMOND

Copyright, Canada, 1957, by
UNIVERSITY OF TORONTO PRESS
Reprinted 2017
ISBN 978-1-4875-9232-5 (paper)

New York: Thomas Nelson & Sons

To Chris

who for eighteen years has taken
in her stride all the vagaries of a
husband-newspaperman,   including
this trip into Communist China

Preface

THIS is not a book in the commonly accepted sense of being a literary composition. It is, rather, a report to the free people of the world on the state of a nation which encompasses a quarter of the earth's population. It is, to the best of my ability as a newspaperman, an unbiased and accurate account of how 650 million Chinese are faring under a Communist regime.

Many of the photographs and of the thousands of words that follow are familiar to readers of the Toronto *Globe and Mail*, since it was for that newspaper the expedition to China was made. The decision to reproduce the results of that trip in this form and thus possibly to reach a wider audience was prompted by the enthusiasm with which the original reports were received by my newspaper's readers, and by the persistent urgings of many good friends, and strangers as well, that my efforts were worthy of being bound in book form.

The trip to Red China was not one I sought, but, like any newspaperman, I would have gladly traded ten years of my life for such an assignment. This sacrifice was not demanded of me by Tommy Munns, the Managing Editor of the *Globe and Mail*. He very casually asked me one day how I would like to go to Red China. The reader of these words does not have to be a newspaperman to appreciate the alacrity with which I replied, "Wonderful."

I am keenly aware that this writing effort does not elevate

me to the select strata occupied by those of my colleagues who have realized the dream of all newspapermen—that of writing the great Canadian novel. But there may be for me the satisfying alternative of having given my readers a realistic peep behind the Bamboo Curtain which has so effectively hidden life in mainland China since control of that part of the world was seized by the Communists in 1949.

The kind co-operation of the Toronto *Globe and Mail* in making available the material upon which this book is based is gratefully acknowledged, as is the pertinacity of the newspaper's Editor and Publisher, Oakley Dalgleish, and Mr. Munns. But for their constant prodding of the author, a procrastinator by nature, it is extremely unlikely that the results of the trip to Red China would now be appearing in this form.

W. K.

Contents

Illustrations

11

NO DOGS IN CHINA

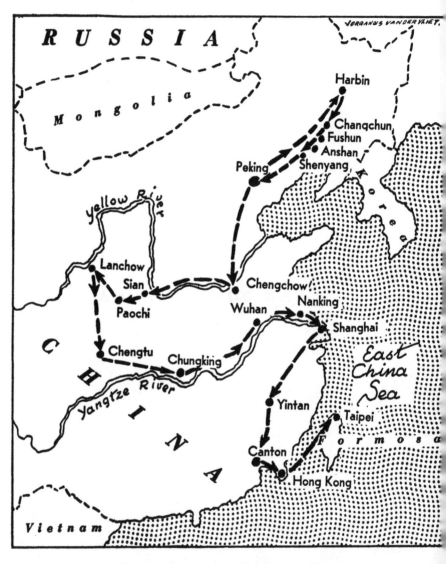

MAP SHOWING AUTHOR'S ITINERARY IN CHINA

CROSSING INTO CHINA

SHUMCHUN. Hardly anyone rides into Red China. Some make their entry into this great unknown country from Moscow. This means an eight-day trip by train, and few Westerners or non-Communists can readily acquire the essential papers for making the journey direct from old-Communist Russia to new-Communist China. The transition from the free world to an ancient country that is being transformed by a Chinese version of Marxism is generally made on foot at this railway station, a pleasant one-hour train ride from Kowloon, which is five minutes by ferry from Hong Kong. As the Bamboo Curtain opened just a crack, to permit the entry of about a hundred persons (half a dozen of them non-Chinese, including two whites), it was perhaps only human to sneak a last glance in the direction of Hong Kong. There lay bright lights, gaiety, music, pretty girls, good food, and comfortable hotels—all the things in life we of the Western world have come to view as commonplace. For myself, the enjoyment of the delights of Hong Kong, a truly magnificent and beautiful city, had been brief—exactly forty-three hours.

My summons to appear at the Chinese Legation in London had been abrupt. It came on a Sunday afternoon and the order was that I was to be in London at 4 P.M. the following Thursday. Strangely, all the rush seemed unimportant and unnecessary as I visited that Thursday afternoon with the Chinese first secretary, Tien Chien, over several cups of tea well laced with jasmine. He quoted from a small diary: "You will be in

China by the 25th!" This was followed by some small chat. As I left, Mr. Tien observed: "You are most fortunate to have had your visa granted so soon." Since I had been waiting for six months for the important document, I was tempted to argue the point but grinned and thought to myself, "Surely not even the Chinese are capable of this kind of humor." After all the urgency of getting to London, it had taken three days to obtain the visa. It is a very pretty thing, in three colors, a unique contribution to a Canadian passport.

From London to Hong Kong is about forty-eight hours by the timetable. It actually takes only thirty-nine hours due to changes in time zones. The trip is a boresome telescoping of time, distance, and, what is most important, food. Regardless of the condition of the stomach, B.O.A.C. feeds by the clock. The world's name places are but a blur. Rome, Istanbul, Karachi, Delhi, Calcutta, and Bangkok are still only names on a map, represented by airports that look just like any other airports. Perhaps two can be described as exceptions— Karachi, because it was about 100 above when we were dumped out onto an apron that felt like a blast furnace, and Bangkok, because in the Thailand capital there was the coolness of dawn in the air.

Hong Kong is now merely a kaleidoscope of hazy memories —a humming harbor of world freighters and Chinese sampans; luxurious houses stretching into the sky and Chinese children reaching out their hands for pennies. Two hours after arriving there, I presented myself at the offices of the China Travel Service, to be informed that the train for China left at 10:15 A.M. Saturday, about forty hours away, and that I should present myself to the Chinese representative in Kowloon at 9:45 A.M. I appeared at the appointed hour. It was duly noted that I had five pieces of luggage. I was presented with a railway ticket from Kowloon to Lowu, the last railway stop outside the Bamboo Curtain. For some reason, as yet unexplained, I was charged an extra $6 for a radio-phone. From there on I was in the hands of the Chinese Travel Service, as it is known in Hong Kong, or China Intourist, as it is called on this side.

It is necessary to walk over a bridge in the transition from one world to another. The last Westerner I saw as I turned sharply to the right into a narrow channel of barbed wire was a British soldier, who grinned and nodded his head at me. To my left was the train to Hong Kong; on my right a train waiting to transport me into China. It is truly a no man's land, for neither train can meet. A roadblock effectively bars this. The first citizens of Red China I saw were two khaki-clad youthful soldiers guarding the entry to their country with tommy-guns.

I was now in the hands of Fong Jet-min, who managed to wrap his Chinese tongue around my name sufficiently well to make it almost understandable. Mr. Fong assisted me with my luggage and we threaded our way to the frontier shed where returning Chinese tourists (frontier people they are called) were going through a skin-searching customs examination. The examiners were poking into a queer assortment of goods—huge vacuum bottles, umbrellas, Chinese foods and sweets, gaily colored clothing. One old woman clutched a beat-up old portable sewing machine under her arm.

We approached the Shumchun railway station on foot through an avenue of pictures. The first was that of Chairman Mao Tse-tung. Then followed an array of pictures of the new China at work and at play. The first impression of the Shumchun railway station was one of complete order. It was, as a matter of fact, a pleasant change from the brief experience of the confusion of Hong Kong and Kowloon with their multiplicity of signs warning against pickpockets and spitting. Here everything conveyed the impression of being under absolute control. It was an orderliness that was refreshing.

There was a cordiality that seemed to be genuine, almost as if the people of this part of China were indeed glad to see a stranger. They demonstrated a desire to please and assist that seemed natural, not an attitude induced by the desire to make a good first impression. Mr. Fong was most attentive. He ushered me into a reception room, poured a cup of green tea, offered a cigaret (Chinese, and excellent smoking) and in short order accomplished this: changed my Hong Kong money for Chinese currency, procured a fan and a cold beer, and ordered lunch.

There were some forms to complete. A customs declaration wanted to know if I was bringing in any sewing machines or accordions, firearms or explosives. The customs examination was cursory. A smartly attired officer, in khaki, glanced briefly at one opened bag and announced: "The procedure is ended."

The train for Canton was scheduled to leave at 12:04 P.M. and it did. The change from the English-style coach with its first-class accommodation (which runs from Kowloon to the border) to a coach which most closely resembles Canada's colonist cars was unexpected. However, I was assured by traveling companions that this constituted de luxe train transportation in China. A later train contained only coaches with bare wooden seats.

As we rolled through the orderly Chinese countryside, with its mosaic of paddies, and women washing clothes in the creeks, our constant companion was the blaring of two loudspeakers, one at either end of the coach, spouting I knew not what. I could only assume it was propaganda. It takes just over three hours to make the trip by train to Canton and we would have had to listen to the screeching for all that time had it not been for a train attendant who thoughtfully disconnected the speaker nearest us. We had then only to listen to the mouthings from the far end of the coach. Whether the attendant did this out of concern for us, or because he was weary of the blather himself, I do not know. But it became somewhat of a game during the trip, since another attendant, possibly more faithful, insisted on plugging the device in again at every opportunity. The contest ended in our favor, since, for most of the trip, we listened only to the muted tones from the rear end of the coach.

IDEOLOGICAL TOUR

CANTON. "Are you Mr. Willie?" This was my introduction to Miss Fen, an indefatigable representative of China Intourist (Chinese Travel Service) who boarded the train seconds after it had creaked into the station amid the blare of propaganda-spouting loudspeakers at exactly 3:15 P.M., the scheduled time of arrival. Miss Fen's error in assuming that my first name was my family name, as is the fashion in China, unfortunately gave me no clue to what lay immediately before me. While I was in the clutches of this highly efficient new-order femininity, I was treated to a whirlwind ride on an ideological merry-go-round that left me weary in mind and body, subconsciously pleading for mercy and almost prepared to roar out the Chinese version of Long Live Peace.

Miss Fen is twenty-three, about five feet, weighs all of eighty pounds, wears glasses equipped with thick lenses, and when I waved good-by to her at the Canton Airport she was still wearing the same squarish brown-and-white gingham dress of the night before. Her white bobby socks and low-heeled shoes did nothing to generate an illusion that she had even a trace of the legendary oriental feminine charm. These vital statistics are not, however, an effective measure of the unbounded energy of this product of the new China whose precise, stilted English was acquired from a textbook at the University of Shanghai.

After my luggage had been gathered together and Miss Fen had apologized for the delay in obtaining a cart to transport it through the platform, due to the tremendous number of visitors China is having, she explained, she parked me in a taxi while she went about the business of clearing me into my first real glimpse of China. It was the wait in the taxi, too, which gave me my first experience of being like a monkey in a zoo. No sooner had I settled down in the back of the car than it was surrounded by a swarm of Chinese—young and old—peering in from all the windows as if they had never seen a white man before. I chanced a grin and it worked. All their faces lighted up in a glow of warmth and I got out of the car only to find myself shaking hands with perhaps a hundred persons. It was a delightful, a warm experience. I had, at last, been welcomed to China.

The welcoming committee, impromptu as it was, was broken up by the arrival of little Miss Fen, who swept them aside, crawled in beside me, and chattered directions to the driver. The drive to what turned out to be a hotel was brief. It was sufficient, however, for me to discover that the normal Canadian manner of speaking would not do. The speech had to be slow and carefully enunciated, or I was liable to lose Miss Fen along the way. As we drove through the streets of Canton in what appeared to be a Ford of the early 1940 period, but which actually was a late-model Polish passenger car, Miss Fen made a little speech in her native sing-song fashion, in which she explained that she really hadn't had much of an opportunity to converse in English. "But how do you think my English is?" she asked. She graced me with a thin smile when I replied, slowly and distinctly, that I hoped

I could be as fluent with Chinese at the end of my visit as she was with my native language.

There was no ceremony of signing the register when we arrived at the hotel. Miss Fen briskly whisked me and my luggage into an elevator, we got off at a floor, and I was ushered into a room. The door was left open and Miss Fen sat down. "What shall we do tonight?" she asked. A question like this, coming from anyone but the efficient Miss Fen, could easily have been misinterpreted. Still somewhat confused by the rush into Red China, I simply shrugged my shoulders and suggested it was up to her. When Miss Fen replied that possibly I should want to rest I readily acquiesced. Glancing at her watch, Miss Fen said it was such and such a time by her and if it was all right with me, she would return in fifteen minutes and take me on a tour of Canton. "What time is your watch, please?" Promptly, in fifteen minutes to the second, Miss Fen was knocking at the door.

It was then the ideological merry-go-round began to spin— with a brief interruption, however. Across from the hotel I spotted what looked like the Canadian equivalent of a milk bar. It really only looked like it. It was an open-front affair (without doors) and I suggested to Miss Fen that perhaps she would care for a cup of coffee. Her response to my offer of hospitality was non-committal. So we went into the Canton version of a milk bar. I don't know yet how it happened but I wound up with a cup of black, thick coffee and a dish of pineapple ice cream. I struggled through both.

Our first stop on the tour of Canton was the memorial to Dr. Sun Yat-sen, who founded the first Chinese republic in 1912. It is a truly magnificent structure, a huge glass-domed auditorium, capable of seating 6,500 people. Sometimes it is used for table tennis tournaments, Miss Fen informed me. The memorial auditorium is set in a large park, at the entrance to which stands a bronze monument of the figure of Dr. Sun.

This, according to Miss Fen, is to be heightened by a considerable number of feet.

Next came a tour of what had been a Confucian temple but is now a national shrine, in which are faithfully reproduced the appurtenances of the Peasants' Training Institute when Chairman Mao was president of it in 1926 and Premier Chou En-lai was a lecturer. I gazed wearily at the bed Chairman Mao had slept on, the desk he had sat at, and the table at which he had dined. There followed in quick succession a glimpse at the Provincial People's Hospital of Kwangtung; the memorial to the Canton Commune, where 8,000 Communists died in a three-day battle with Kuomintang forces in December, 1927; and the Pearl River bridge, destroyed by the retreating Nationalist forces in October, 1948, and since rebuilt.

The merry-go-round stopped briefly for dinner, during which I was left to my own devices. In the course of it I was initiated into the game of three matches to see who pays for the beer by a group of business men which included an Englishman, a Dane, a German, a Swede, and a Pole, all strangers to me. Strangely enough, I didn't lose.

Promptly at 8 o'clock Miss Fen was knocking on the door and off we walked (but not arm in arm) to the Canton Culture Park, a sort of Chinese version of a midway with plenty of ideology thrown in. It was a pleasant relief, in a way, to watch the puppet show, a demonstration of magic, and even to stroll through the buildings and view the displays of the products of modern China. There was even the skeleton of what Miss Fen claimed to be the world's biggest fish. As the crackle of fireworks mingled with the jangle of a Chinese band, I suggested we return to the hotel, keenly aware that I would have to be up at 5:00 A.M. in order to catch a 6:15 plane.

Canton, the home of about 1,700 thousand, richly deserves the sobriquet attached to it by previous visitors of being the noisiest city in the world. It was difficult to determine just when night ended and morning began. The city was a ferment of noise at all hours. The Canton symphony, which made a mockery of attempts to sleep, was highlighted by the strident bleats of boat whistles signaling their approach to the Pearl River bridge. It mattered not, it seemed, that the bridge had not opened its jaws since its destruction and subsequent re-building eight years ago. The force of habit is strong, especially among rivermen. In between whistles were blended bicycle bells, the yells of pedicab drivers warning all to get out of their way; the laughter and the cries of children who seemed never to go to sleep; the screaming of tires as Canton's handful of motor vehicles darted around corners.

As we turned into the airport at 6:00 next morning, my one open eye glimpsed a group of about a hundred flower-bearing children, dressed in gaily colored costumes, lined up by the entrance. "So nice of you to arrange this farewell for me," I suggested to Miss Fen. Alas, it turned out that they were waiting to greet Russian President Voroshilov on his way to Peking for the May Day celebrations.

SKYSCRAPERS AND PAGODAS

PEKING. The nine-hour trip from Canton by air, including brief stops at Wuhan and Chengchow, was made in a Russian version of the Convair, a comfortable aircraft which traveled most of the time at about 8,000 feet. Except for the absence of seat belts and a clock where the "fasten seat belts—no smoking" warnings should be, the plane was very much like its Canadian counterpart and the trip as uneventful as a routine flight in Canada.

According to the local version of a Chamber of Commerce, this capital city of China is both a very old and a very new city. Nowhere is this more evident than from above. As the plane dipped in from the northwest on the approach to the city, it passed over the Great Wall of China and followed the Peking-Paotow railway line past the Temple of Sleeping Buddha, the Temple of Azure Clouds, and the Summer Palace, the playground of the emperors of the Manchu dynasty. These truly represented the something old in Peking. The something new was represented by square red and gray blocks that abruptly thrust themselves out of the broad expanse of dull, grayish, one-story buildings. These were the multitude of new government buildings and of new rows of workers' flats which are sprouting all over this ancient city. From the air the suburbs gave the same impression of mushroom growth as is to be found on the outskirts of any Canadian city. Even at several thousand feet it was impossible to escape the feeling that here was a city in a frenzy of activity, trying to do in a few years what other cities have done in centuries.

It seems the first impulse of a totalitarian government is to erect splendid public buildings as if, somehow, they are a symbol of the might of the people. Thus it has been the fate of Peking to have its symmetrical skyline of graceful pagoda roofs and beautiful and historical temple gates gashed by modern medium-sized skyscrapers, built apparently to no particular plan but erected in a hurry and just as quickly occupied. Perhaps this has been the lot of Peking because it is again the capital of China. On three earlier occasions, as far back as the Yuan (Mongol) dynasty (1279–1368) and as recently as the Ching (Manchu) dynasty (1644–1911), Peking has been the national capital. It had not, however, acquired the massive structures generally associated with capital cities.

Since 1949, when the Communists overran China and proclaimed Peking again China's capital, the Mao regime has feverishly attempted to find working space for the huge government machinery needed to manage the affairs of more than 600 million people. Most of the buildings are utilitarian in design and construction and the actual speed of erection is startling. All the work is done by hand, yet new buildings, enclosed in a latticework of bamboo scaffolding, grow appreciably daily. Indicating the haste with which the new order in China demanded erection of government buildings are some of those built in the early months after 1949. They abjectly wear their pagoda roofs as if testifying to the reluctance of China's architects to part completely with the past. Buildings completed in recent years are in the flat-roof mode. Some conception of the building activity in recent years is given in a statistical report on the city. It states that between 1949 (the year from which everything is dated in present-day China) and 1955, new buildings had a total floor space of 10,744,000 square yards, equivalent to 70 per cent of the floor space of all the buildings that were standing in 1949.

Among these new structures are three new hotels, the Peace, the Hsinchiao, and the Chien Men; hostels for foreign technicians, generally occupied by Russian experts and located on the outskirts of the city; and a special transit hostel for Chinese who have returned from overseas. It was to the Chien Men that I was escorted on my arrival here by Yen Pao-chiu, the third Chinese Intourist interpreter to make himself responsible for my movements this side of the Bamboo Curtain. The Chien Men, three years old, is one of the larger hotels, located in the outer city to the south. It is M-shaped and has a central building eight stories high and two six-storied wings. It can accommodate about four hundred guests. Since it is the favorite haunt of good-will delegates, and China plays host to thousands of them annually, its comparative newness is not apparent. Rather there is a down-at-the-heels atmosphere accentuated by the unhappy fact that nothing really works well in the hotel. Taps drip, leaving stains in sinks and tubs; toilets run constantly and sometimes tanks overflow; doors do not fit properly; light bulbs glow glimly, aggravating a perpetual nightly dimout prompted by a power shortage.

Ensconced as I was on the seventh floor of this modern hotel, in a city of 4 million people, it was indeed strange to find myself being awakened by the crowing of a rooster. The cock-a-doodle-doo greeting the dawn would not have seemed at all incongruous in Canton, but I came to realize that all Canton's noises except the boat whistles were prevalent in Peking, only more so. As I peered out the window, searching for the source of the crowing, I could see, dimly outlined by the early morning light, the Yenshan Mountains beyond which lies the famed Great Wall. Also within easy seeing distance were the Gate of Heavenly Peace, the Gate of Supreme Harmony, and Longevity Hill. It was on a rickety wood-wire fence which separated the hotel lawn from one of the narrow, winding, packed-earth, lanelike streets along which Peking's teeming millions live that I saw the cause of the early-morning commotion. It was a rooster and a few yards away a dozen hens scratching for their breakfast.

Here was another illustration of Peking's blend of the new and the old. Here were living its people, as they have lived for thousands of years, crowded together, perhaps forty to the space occupied by a five-room bungalow in a North American city. Within these rows of one-story, dingy, brick dwellings, facing in on courtyards, generations have been born, have lived, and have died, raising their chickens, unconcerned and unmoved by the fever of construction activity all around them, except when whole rows of their poor houses are swept into the discard to make room for a government building or a wide boulevard, as has frequently happened. Here, in China's metropolis, they continue to raise their chickens in their homes, and traffic along the mud sidewalks is just as likely to consist of flocks of fowl as of rosy-cheeked children, all of whose noses seem always to need wiping, or pig-tailed young lasses hop-skipping their way to school.

HANDY POCKET INTERPRETER

PEKING. The first few days after the entry through the Bamboo Curtain, while baffling because of the total absence of anything in English, are eased for the newcomer by the ever-present Intourist representative. In fact, one gets to feel something like an infant in transit from one country to another and being passed from one hand to another. All one lacks is a lapel tag giving name, age, and the name of the person who will accept delivery. While in the care of Intourist, which arranges transportation, hotel, meals, and cars, there is a comfortable if somewhat strange feeling of security. It might almost be described as a state of somnolent happiness—not a care in the world. It is when the Intourist nurse departs that China becomes a frightening place, a foreign and alien country. There is not a soul to talk to and, what is far worse, there is seemingly no way of making one's requirements known.

It is extremely difficult for an outsider to guess the age of Chinese people, so it came as somewhat of a shock when I learned that Yen Pao-chiu, my Peking guide, is thirty-one, married, and has one child. He looks about twenty. His English, acquired at the University of Peking, is a refreshing change from the precise mouthings of Miss Fen in Canton. He is understandable, but he has the charming inability of the Chinese to pronounce "l" and "r" and quite often he has trouble with "k" and "a." This, added to his consternation when the English he hears comes too quickly for him, makes for an amusing confusion. He was late arriving at the airport and breathlessly spilled out an explanation which indicated that the plane had arrived ahead of schedule; he apologized for having kept me waiting all of five minutes.

Apparently it is not necessary for guests in China to register at hotels. I am now staying at my fourth Chinese hotel and have only recently discovered that their only record of me is a letter from China Intourist requesting accommodation for one visitor. Before leaving me on my first night in Peking, Mr. Yen obtained for me the telephone number of an English news agency correspondent here and left with me the Intourist telephone number. It was after Mr. Yen had departed that I had my worst moment of panic. I suddenly realized that I didn't know where I was. He had not given me the name of the hotel. After considerable fiddling with the dial telephone, which has no letters, I discovered that it was necessary to dial O before trying the number, which had five digits. The speed with which Intourist supplied the hotel name and telephone number was reassuring.

A newcomer's first few ventures into the byways of Peking can be most confusing. The natural inclination in a strange city is to study the nearest intersection and attempt to retain a mental picture of it as a guide on the return trip. This is all very well except that in Peking all intersections appear to look alike and, in fact, do. It was only the height of the hotel and its roof-top array of brilliant red flags flapping in the breeze that kept me from losing my way. That meant that I moved in a constricted area, since there are many buildings in this city of the same height, similar appearance, and all sporting the same red-flag decoration.

I eventually resorted to the device of carrying around little slips of paper on which Mr. Yen, my interpreter, had written, in Chinese characters and in English, names and addresses of such places as the hotel, the Chinese Foreign Office (a frequent port of call for foreign correspondents), the British Legation, and others. Some Chinese understand a few words of English but they are few and far between and not always available to help instruct a pedicab driver or enlighten a traffic constable who understands nothing of what is being asked of him. The bilingual direction slips were indeed a most valuable contribution to easing traveling in this city. Meals are no problem so long as eating is confined to the hotels. A fair attempt is made to provide European-style food as a change from Chinese, which is all that can be obtained outside the hotels, and menus are printed in English, Russian, and Chinese. In their attempts to vary the diet of visitors and to interpret some English expressions, the Chinese have made some peculiar linguistic excursions. I was somewhat taken aback one noon to see "hot prawn balls" listed. They turned out to be fried shrimps. "Moose" was, as suspected, mousse, and an eager waiter one morning urged me to have some "hotty dogs."

The furious anti-foreign wave which swept this country in 1949 not only resulted in the disappearance of all English road signs, but also, to the occasional embarrassment of foreigners, left no way of determining which public washroom is the right one. In hotels and airports this is rarely a problem since in those places washrooms are identified in English and Russian. The personal problem of knowing which door to enter where there was no obvious clue was solved by carrying around another little slip of paper, carefully secreted in my press card, on which were inscribed the Chinese characters for MEN.

The absence of English as a written language is also reflected in a paucity of reading material. There are available, for the asking, volumes of publications turned out by China's foreign language press which extol in somewhat naive English the virtues of the revolution and what has been accomplished for China by the Communists since 1949. For those who quickly weary of a constant diet of all praise to Chairman Mao and curses on the imperialists and war lords there is on Morrison Street, the main street of Peking, a literary sanctuary known as the Guozi Shudian, the International Bookstore. This, too, has more than its share of propaganda efforts, most of them in Russian and the languages of other countries which maintain diplomatic relations with China. But there is one slight difference—a small corner which, at this distance, seems a delight to the English-hungry traveler. Here can be found an amazing variety of books in English; amazing because of the varied subject matter. For three or four Chinese yuan (a Canadian dollar is roughly equivalent to 2½ yuan) there are these titles from which to choose: *The Truman Era*; *Modern Chinese Stories*; *The National Question in Kerula*; *All Quiet on the Western Front*; *Elementary Spanish Conversation*; *Intermediate Portuguese Conversation*; *Egyptian Colloquial Arabic*; *Introduction to Scandinavian Literature*; *Spanish Self-Taught*; Theodore Dreiser's *The Stoic*; *Eastern Europe in the Socialist World* by Hewlett Johnson (the Red Dean of Canterbury); *Bernard Shaw: His Life, Work, and Friends*; Emile Zola's *Zest for Life*; *Outline of Political History of the Americas*; *Tom Sawyer*; a life of Abraham Lincoln; and several books by Thomas Mann.

Across the street there is the Tung An Bazaar, spread across ten acres occupied by about 600 small stalls and stores. This huge merchandising center is hidden behind the walls of other buildings and is scarcely visible from the outside streets, where there are a few, not easily noticeable, entrances. The bazaar offers all manner of articles but the main stress is on the specialties of Peking—curios and objets d'art, handicrafts, old books, and preserved fruits. Here, too, can be purchased books in English, but the Tung An Bazaar has its own curious collection: *Elements of Utility Rate Deterioration*; *Budgeting Control*; a January 19, 1951, copy of the *Electrical Review*, an

English publication, price one shilling; a life of William Booth, founder of the Salvation Army, in two volumes; a February 2, 1935, copy of the English magazine the *Sphere*. One may also purchase for 300 yuan an ancient family Bible, in English. There was no printed date to give a clue to its age, which might be 100 years from the brittleness of its dust-encrusted thick leather covers. Nor was there any clue to who, in China, had used it, since there was not even a pen scratch on the pages headed "Family Register."

CAPITALISTS CAPITULATE

PEKING. The Communist party—which in reality is China's government, since, with one or two minor exceptions, top government officials are also senior party members—is constantly singing the praises of Soviet Russia but it is not loth to profit by Russia's mistakes. It is true that the words of Lenin, Marx, and Stalin are used to decide an ideological dispute. Marxism is the creed of new China as it is of Russia. But the government and the party, since the two are inseparable, are prepared to compromise with pure Marxism in applying it to conditions that are peculiar to China.

Thus we find that whereas Communist China has, as its ultimate goal, state ownership of all of the means of production—everything shall belong to the people—it has compromised with Marxism to the extent of establishing a system of state capitalism. It is not attempting, as was the case in Russia, to immediately swallow all industrial activities. In the name of expediency (a course of action which has the official blessing of Chairman Mao Tse-tung, who has frequently qualified the strict application of Marxist theory to China by saying "in China and in present circumstances") the government now finds itself in partnership with private enterprise. It is a system of joint ownership in which, admittedly, the government has the final say, but which permits the payment of annual dividends to owners and shareholders.

The details of this private-state ownership system were outlined for me by Wu Chang Ming, who is chief of the Bureau of Commerce and Industry. In the course of the interview Mr. Wu also supplied, at my request, the Chinese definition of what exactly constitutes a capitalist, since it is now such a nasty word in China, on the same low level as imperialist, warlord, and feudal landlord. So far, then, as the Chinese government is concerned, a capitalist is a person who has more than 2,000 yuan invested in a business or property. That's about $800 in Canadian currency.

Some of these Chinese capitalists fell by the wayside during the hectic first years of the revolution when any person with the appearance of affluence was suspected of being an enemy of the people. Those who survived now find themselves in a dual position. They still retain a property interest in their trades, receiving an annual percentage on the assets they turned into the partnership. But since their enterprises are now managed as part of China's planned economy, they are also salaried government employees. The men who have entered into this partnership with the government—and they included just about all private industry in China, since an employer becomes a candidate for partnership if he hires four or more people—are left under no illusion as to their future.

The government views the present system which went into effect in 1955 as having a life of seven years. It will terminate at the end of China's second five-year economic development plan which was launched this year. The position of the capitalists is perhaps best described by Ho Shan-huei, deputy chief of the economic department of the Chinese daily *Ta Kung Pao*, who put it this way: "This double status is, of course, temporary. In future, the capitalists will have only one capacity. When the transition to Socialism is completed they will be workers in a completely publicly-owned economy. And their income will consist wholly of the wages or salaries they earn."

At the moment, about 190,000 businesses are operated as joint private-and-state-ownership enterprises. About 44,000 are industrial, 97,000 commercial; in the rest are included hotels, restaurants, and other services. These will become completely state-owned and operated by 1962 unless, as is entirely possible, the Chinese again bend theory to expediency.

Although the new approach to private enterprise became official government policy in 1955, conversion was slow. It was not until 1956 that there came the high tide of transformation, and thousands of private industrialists practically begged the government to come in as a partner. The official explanation given by Mr. Wu for this eagerness of private enterprisers to join forces with the government is that they had grown with the times. They perceived (and the expression is Mr. Wu's) that Socialism held prosperity and a future for all citizens. "They discovered Socialism," Mr. Wu said. "In the years since the liberation they had acquired a social consciousness."

This awakening on the part of the private enterpriser was given an assist by the government, which opened schools for capitalists. There is now a Socialist college in this city which is designed purely for the transformation of capitalists. There are many processes, apparently, through which the so-called capitalist goes before he emerges eager to participate in the Socialist revolution. The Chinese are now even prepared to admit that brainwashing is perhaps an apt description of the processing. In addition to the mental readjustment which brings about a change of heart, Mr. Wu did not hesitate to admit that a certain degree of economic pressure hastens the rate of transformation. Those capitalists who resisted the urge to become partners in 1955 (and there were many) discovered to their financial sorrow that they were going bankrupt.

Most of China's peasants had been enlisted in state co-operatives; the working force was attracted to government-owned industry by higher wages and better working conditions. As good Socialists, both peasants and workers preferred to buy from state stores and made their selection from goods manufactured by state companies. This loyalty also influenced the peasants in disposing of their surplus produce, that which they were permitted to retain after the co-operative had taken its share in the name of the state and the common good. Naturally, they were inclined to sell only to state agencies. Squeezed between a lack of customers and having to pay higher prices for material purchased in a restricted free market, the unrepentant private enterpriser found himself in a most uncompetitive position. In the words of Mr. Wu, his transition to Socialism became voluntary, often enthusiastic.

Government policy on posts for capitalists is: "Jobs according to ability, and proper consideration for all." It is admitted that many of these people have a good knowledge of engineering or business administration, so they generally become managers or assistant managers in their own plants or in companies formed by the merger of several smaller plants. The government's interests are safeguarded by a representative who may also be an assistant manager, in which capacity he is also expected to do a full day's work.

Until the end of 1955, the profits of joint state-private enterprises were divided into four roughly equal parts which went to tax payments, reserve funds, workers' welfare, and dividends to shareholders. This system has now been scrapped, and replaced by a 5 per cent annual interest guaranteed by the state to all shareholders regardless of the profit or loss of individual units. This interest is paid quarterly, and is based on the valuation given by owners and shareholders which, of course, is finally confirmed by government auditors. Distribution to shareholders is made by those who were responsible for this duty while the enterprises were still privately owned. Shareholders in Hong Kong and abroad are also paid; if their address is unknown the money is banked here in trust for them.

Just about all of China's industrial capacity is now operated wholly by the state or under this state capitalism. And, lest the former private enterprisers should be inclined to backslide into un-Marxian views, they are still being politically educated through courses that deal with the resources and history of China, the history of China's revolution and Communist party, basic policies in the transition to Socialism, the history of human society, and the birth, development and decline of capitalism as a system.

INVITATION TO CRITICISM

PEKING. The Chinese government now feels assured that it has successfully completed one phase in its march toward a fully Communist economy. This period is that which involved the use of force against those considered by the government to be counter-revolutionaries or enemies of the state. This is the interpretation by observers here of a lengthy statement issued by Chou Yang, vice-director of the central propaganda department of the Communist party. The party's propaganda machine is used to condition the people well in advance for government policy changes. Mr. Chou's announcement, which was made publicly at a specially summoned conference of representatives of the foreign press, said in effect that the party no longer fears an attack by an internal enemy. He admitted that there are probably still a few counter-revolutionaries in existence but added that they are no longer considered a menace by the party.

The announcement also brought into proper perspective articles in the Chinese newspapers dealing with "contradictions" within the party itself. The expression "contradiction" is a favorite with Communists and particularly with Chairman Mao, who gave a long lecture on the subject in 1937 at the anti-Japanese military political college in Yenan. The lecture has since been reprinted several times in pamphlet form and is included in a volume known as the *Selected Works of Mao Tse-tung* which is, to some extent, a Chinese Communist manifesto. According to Chairman Mao, contradiction is universal, absolute, existing in all processes of the development of things and running through all processes from beginning to end.

The current newspaper discussion of contradictions within the party and within the ranks of the people of China, Mr. Chou explained, is in furtherance of a direction by Chairman Mao last year that "a hundred flowers should bloom and a hundred schools of thought contend." In other words, the Communist regime now feels it is so securely entrenched in China that it is prepared to welcome criticism and that critics do not need to fear they will be the victims of harsh repressive measures.

This is not to say, however, that criticisms of party policy will be permitted. There is no indication of any departure from the democratic centralism which has always been the guiding rule of the Chinese Communist party. This policy means that, in theory, party members at all levels may debate policy freely until policy is decided. Once a decision has been reached all members must close ranks and accept it.

What is apparently happening now is that party members and the people as a whole are being invited to criticize the application of these policies. They are to be permitted to draw to the attention of the authorities instances where misapplication of a policy is jeopardizing the forward progress of China to a Communist state.

One of the main "contradictions," one that seems to be giving the Communists considerable concern, is the difference in living standards between the workers and the peasants and between peasants in one part of the country and those in another. The *People's Daily*, one of China's most widely circulated newspapers, has just published the results of two economic surveys conducted by the government which clearly illustrate the problem now being faced by the regime. One survey, which covered 56,000 families in Kiangsu province, which includes Shanghai, disclosed that last year the average family income was 455 yuan or about $182 Canadian. By contrast, a similar survey of 1,000 families in Kansu province, in northwest China, showed the average annual income to be 171 yuan ($69 Canadian). The difference is not so great as the figures would indicate, since the cost of living would be somewhat lower in Kansu province, but the disparity is still sufficient to worry a party which owes its present position as the government of China to the support of the peasants.

Mr. Chou explained that now that the first phase of the revolution, the one in which all criticism must be treated as antagonistic—that is, between friend and foe—has come to an end, the party, in its own interests, must devote itself to an attempt to satisfy the material needs of the people. Mr. Chou frankly admitted that if the party failed to reflect the interests of the people in it, and of those over whom it exercises control, it was in danger of being cast aside. He did not suggest that the party feels this is a prospect it needs to fear.

In the same frank vein, Mr. Chou said there must necessarily, for the foreseeable future at least, be differences in living standards in various parts of China, due mainly to the fact that China is still a poor country. But it is necessary, he stressed, that there should not be too big a difference. The living standards should not be too far apart. There is an old Chinese proverb, Mr. Chou added, that says: "Be not afraid of not having enough, but of unequal distribution of what you have." In pursuance of the spirit of this proverb, Mr. Chou cautioned that the Chinese Communists are not egalitarians but they feel the difference should be as small as possible. He recalled that when a food shortage had existed after the 1949 revolution, the government policy at that time had been that the food of two should be shared by three. In effect, he implied, the present crisis, if it can be so described, is to be solved by a continuance of government policy that "what we have should be shared by everyone."

THE PARTY AND THE INTELLECTUALS

PEKING. It is a fact that all through the long history of China the lasting governments were those that had the confidence and support of both the peasants and the intellectuals. Administrations that ignored this maxim were short-lived. So the present government of China, a Communist regime which fought its way to power with the aid of a peasant army of one million and the active support of peasants throughout this vast country, is paying some heed to the historical value of having the enthusiastic support of the scholars—the intellectuals. The Chinese Communist party is wooing the country's intellectuals. It is publicly assuring them that they can now say whatever they wish. The intellectuals, if they feel so inclined, may put forward non-Marxist views without fearing that they will be the victims of repressive measures.

This is another phase of the current Communist party campaign of inviting constructive criticism of its administration. It is, as Chou Yang, vice-director of the party's central propaganda department, explained, a policy of rectifying an earlier stand taken by the party—one of fear of all public criticism. "Our policy now is to let the flowers and the weeds bloom together," Mr. Chou explained. "There is, we must admit, some apprehension on the part of party members but this is being eliminated. We are trying to persuade them that if you prevent weeds growing you also prevent flowers blooming. Without criticism there can be no new ideas."

The Communist party spokesman frankly admitted that this new policy of letting the flowers and the weeds bloom together is being viewed with some skepticism by the intellectuals. He also acknowledged that past treatment by the party of the country's intellectuals justified their present reluctance to accept the invitation to voice their criticisms in the open. "There were shortcomings after the liberation," Mr. Chou said. "The remolding of the intellectuals was carried out in a relatively rough way. There was not sufficient thought given to the problem. In some places the method used was too simple, too rough. It is not to be wondered that the intellectuals now feel slightly uncomfortable." Mr. Chou did not detail the rough methods he had in mind but it is well documented that for a few years after 1949 the Communists applied literally the official party attitude toward intellectuals as given in a lecture at Yenan in 1942 by Chairman Mao. He said then ". . . Marxism-Leninism . . . will destroy any brand of creative spirit which is not of the masses and of the proletariat. . . . they should be extirpated to make room for the new."

Many of China's intellectuals bowed to the inevitable and

accepted the new Communist ideals although many reserved the right to grumble in private. When the Communists demanded more of them in 1951, about 15,000 writers and artists publicly announced that they had become genuinely Marxist in their outlook. This they did as the consequence of persistent nagging and persuasion by the Communists. This approach, which has resulted in what Mr. Chou described as an ideological remolding of intellectuals, is now to be discarded. Mr. Chou was quite candid as to the results of the remolding campaigns, even though he deplored the methods which had been used. Admitting that despite all the party's efforts it had still not been able to completely convert all of China's intellectuals, Mr. Chou said that one result of the ideological remolding is that even those intellectuals who have refused to become party members are now able to distinguish between friend and foe. They support such basic Communist efforts as land reform.

Now China's intellectuals can say whatever they wish, Mr. Chou declared. Any apprehensions they may still feel are to be swept away by the Communist party's assurance that what happened immediately after 1949 is in the past. The party has explained it won't happen again. "Wrong ideas," Mr. Chou said, "will be criticized in a gentle way as with a fine rain and a soft breeze. We will not return to the old methods of criticizing the intellectuals."

In this new soft approach to the country's intelligentsia, observers here see an assurance on the part of the Communists that the intellectual leaders of the nation have now been rendered harmless. The Communists no longer fear that the hundreds of thousands of graduates of new China's mass education program are likely to be wrongly influenced and directed by totally unreformed intellectuals simply because such people no longer exist. The peace-with-the-intellectuals-move is also interpreted as being a belated realization by the Communists that they need the wholehearted co-operation of the intelligentsia if the rapid industrialization of China, commenced with the first five-year plan, is to be maintained and continued through the second five-year plan, which began this year.

It is also a recognition that the intellectuals left over from the time of the 1949 revolution have a contribution to make to the economy. The value of this is being destroyed by over-enthusiastic implementation of Chairman Mao's 1942 views on the future of the intelligentsia. So it is that over-eager young Marxists in the party are now being cautioned to take it easy. In their Marxist evaluation of the country's older scientists, professors, artists, etc., they are being told not to ignore the achievements of these people before the revolution and the acknowledged contributions they have made since that date.

RED TAPE

PEKING. In their current "anti-contradiction" campaign, the Communists of China are not overlooking their own members, and are paying particular attention to the cadres, the mainstay of this country's political system. The term "contradiction," as it applies to party members, can be taken as meaning doctrinairism, subjectivism, and bureaucracy, all of which, the party leaders feel, are endangering the course of the revolution now that it can safely be assumed that the armed phase of the revolution has come to an end. As the party sees it, the danger of members becoming victims of these three contradictions is that they will fail to adapt themselves to changing conditions.

It is frankly admitted by party heads that China has suffered greatly from doctrinairism simply because the Chinese, lacking experience in Socialism, looked to Russia as a guide. "We must learn from Russia; it is always a step ahead of us," they still say in China. But, this seemingly bland acceptance of all that is Russian as being good does not actually reflect the true attitude of the Chinese, which is that they must also learn from countries opposed to the Chinese political system. This attitude is expressed to some extent by the familiar Chinese Communist expression: "Our problem is how to know how to learn well."

The cadre is a political phenomenon peculiar to China. In its strictest sense the word means nucleus or framework, and in China the cadre is an individual who is a dedicated party servant. He is the backbone of the party. Many of the cadres are graduates of a training school established by the Communists when they were participating with the Kuomintang in a united front against the Japanese. Candidates had to be young and enthusiastic and willing to give themselves completely to party service. Loyalty, obedience, initiative, and ability in organizing masses are the qualities chiefly required of the cadres and they proved their value to the party at the time of the revolution in 1949 when 150,000 of them were ready to move into liberated areas to establish some system of government.

One basic part of the early training of cadres was that they learn from other sections of society. This meant that those from the worker and peasant classes had to take courses on cultural matters. Those with an adequate intellectual background went to live with the peasants so they could learn their language and acquaint themselves with their problems. Today many cadres are civil servants and many political leaders at lower levels are cadres.

The party leaders now feel that these people are developing into a bureaucracy, a trend inherent in all totalitarian forms of government. So now the party is engaged in an ideological remolding of its leading cadres. "This is sometimes described as brainwashing," said Chou Yang, vice-director of the central propaganda department of the Chinese Communist party. "That is what it is. We need to wash our faces every day, why shouldn't our brains be washed? Brains must be washed to adjust to changes in the world." The brains of the Communist party are being washed through the simple expedient of putting the cadres out to do some hard toil. This the Communists described as the process of rectification. It is another example of ideological remolding being done through argument and persuasion rather than through force.

This current brainwashing reflects the realization by the party that if it doesn't reflect the interests of the people it becomes a bureaucratic organization, a danger to its own existence no matter how strong it may appear to be. The party, while admitting the existence within it of bureaucrats, insists that they are hard-working but that they are not now sufficiently concerned about the interests of the masses. "They are relying solely on commands or using force," Mr. Chou explained. "They are not able to see the problems. There is not enough concern about the interests of the masses."

This interest is now to be rekindled through a process of exposure to actual conditions. The cadres are going to be put to work, some of it physical work. The decision was an important one, Mr. Chou explained. "The decision was made because it takes work to build socialism, a great deal of physical work. Intellectual work is secondary. The cadres must make closer ties with the workers and the peasants. Only through physical work can they merge with them." Apparently grumblings from the peasant level of Chinese society assisted party chiefs in arriving at this important decision.

The work test is to be first applied at the village level, where it was first realized that cadres were losing contact with everyday problems. The chairmen of co-operatives ceased to work in the fields, and other peasants were prompted into comments such as: "So they are scholars now, not peasants."

In putting the cadres back to work the Communists are running into a serious problem at the provincial and central government levels. Most of these cadres are in the forty-to-fifty age group. The problem is how to put them to hard work, since it will most likely be work on the roads or digging ditches or shoveling earth. "We will have to use caution," Mr. Chou said. "It will not be a paying proposition if half a day's hard work puts a cadre in hospital for a month."

There is to be no compulsion in this back-to-work movement for the cadres. It will be a purely voluntary movement recommended by the party because it will help to change their way of thinking.

SPEED-UP OF ENGINEERS' TRAINING

PEKING. "We can't wait; we are a nation in a hurry!" The speaker was Chang Chiun, China's director of planning for higher education. As we talked, we strolled through the beautiful grounds of the Imperial Gardens, thirty-five acres of lush greenery and shrubbery, set aside 800 years ago as a place where advisers to the Ming dynasty could dwell leisurely upon matters of state. Now the serenity of the scenic beauty is marred by a grotesque eight-story building erected during the Japanese occupation and now used as the Ministry headquarters. Another large piece has been carved out of the gardens for a more utilitarian purpose—a basketball field for the staff and a drill ground for the twice-daily setting-up exercises that the new China expects of all government employees.

China fully expects to be a modern state in every respect in 1967 at the end of its third five-year plan, when its economy will be converted from one which is now predominantly agricultural (64 per cent) to a highly industrialized state where agriculture will be relegated to a 35 per cent share; but, as a nation in a hurry, she has made some errors. These are frankly admitted. One was in borrowing from Russia the short-course procedure of training engineers.

"The People's Government," Mr. Chang explained, "decided we must speed up the development of higher education, especially the technical end of it. Time did not permit us to give student engineers the regular four or five years of university training that they had previously been receiving. We thought that because the short course was in use in Russia it would suit our purposes. We thought it would give us the engineers we needed in a hurry," Mr. Chang observed. "We developed engineers very quickly; the rate of increase since 1949 has been about 20 per cent annually and from 1949 to 1956 we graduated 302,000 engineers, about half of whom had taken the special two-year course." It just didn't work, Mr. Chang sadly commented, and now all engineer students are on four- or five-year courses. The folly of this attempt to cram the teaching of five years into two years soon became apparent. The two-year courses were abandoned at the end of 1955 when a stocktaking disclosed that although 6,000 geologists, for instance, had been graduated from the short courses in the three years from 1952 to 1954, almost all of them were fit only to be assistants to the handful of properly trained geologists then available in China.

The policy of concentrating on numbers rather than quality came in for some sharp criticism by government officials which prompted a hasty reorganization of higher education. In an interim report on the first five-year plan, which ends this year, Li Fu-chun, vice-premier of the state council and chairman of the state planning commission, said: "The tendency to go after numbers only and ignore quality is clearly not in the interests of the state plan of construction. The higher engineering institutes have already begun to feel that the number of students increased too rapidly while the standards of learning and skill of the students are not high enough." Factories and mines, Mr. Li commented, had complained that higher professional standards must be demanded of technical personnel during training. "From now on we must pay keen attention to the standards demanded of students."

One way in which the Chinese educationists attempted to telescope the engineering course was by eliminating foreign languages, reducing the time spent on arithmetic, physics and chemistry, and field work. They were also reminded by Mr. Li of another very important omission in a totalitarian regime: "We must see to it that the technical personnel are politically reliable," he suggested. This was just as important, he said, as competence, an adequate knowledge of modern science and technology, and good health.

Premier Chou En-lai, reporting on the second five-year plan to get under way next year, had this to say on the subject: "In order to improve the work of training personnel for construction, we must pay due consideration to the relation between numbers and quality. In the past few years we have put undue emphasis on numbers and neglected quality; this is a tendency which must be corrected." And corrected it was. It was speedily announced that the Ministry of Higher Education had revised the enrollment plan in higher educational institutions for the last three years of the first planned period. It had also decided to replace, by stages and within two or three years, the four-year system in engineering colleges with the five-year system and gradually abolish the two- and three-year special courses.

It was sheer necessity, Mr. Chang explained, that prompted his department to subject itself to government criticism. The department bowed to the demands of the construction program and a nation in which everybody seemed to be in a hurry: so much so that students poured into new school buildings before they could be completed and lived and studied while workmen were still adding the finishing touches.

The clash between the two desires—quantity and quality —has not yet been resolved, and the question is still the subject of a great deal of controversy as to what shall be the final shape of China's engineering educational system. The country is still aiming at producing specialized graduates able to do an engineer's work in their particular field on graduation. Now a group of educators contend that this is not the best way. They hold that the students ought to concentrate more on basic theoretical studies so as to foster their ability to think for themselves. Opposed to this idea are those who feel that China's immediate and overriding need is for technicians trained for a particular job, however limited their over-all knowledge.

Both schools of thought, however, are agreed on the value of an experiment now being tried at the various colleges. Third-year engineering students do six to eight weeks' work in a factory as part of their training, with the idea that they should get the feel of the actual job, applying what they have learned in the classroom and gaining practical experience that will be of help in their further studies. This production practice, as it is called, has the Ministry's approval as long as it does not cause too great organizational difficulties for the factories involved.

TEACHING THE TEACHERS

PEKING. One reform the Communists immediately concerned themselves with after they seized power in 1949 was the reformation of curricula in accordance with their own view of the needs of the Chinese people in a Communist economy. It was required, the Communists decreed, that education be national, scientific, and popular; that it be linked with the tasks of national construction in the service of the people; and that its methods unite theory and practice. The first targets of the Communists were the teachers, who, in a self-education campaign, were asked to examine and reassess their attitudes, ideas, and methods in the light of the needs of a Communist state. The duties of a teacher who has been ideologically remolded are clearly defined by the Communists: he must see to it that the students comprehend the subjects he is teaching; their demand for learning must be satisfied; failing to help them master the course means failure in the duty of a teacher.

One method adopted by the Communists to keep the profession on its toes was to introduce the custom of having teachers in the same pedagogic research group give trial lectures before their colleagues. In this way they could judge what errors needed to be corrected and what improvements should be made. It is the pedagogic research group that draws up the teaching program or outline of courses. Since they are the collective output of the groups, the programs and outlines must be adhered to by every teacher. Initially, the Communists admit, the teachers considered it preposterous for one teacher to offer advice to another, especially a senior one. Having, presumably, been effectively remolded in their thinking, all teachers were expected to accept collective preparation for lecturing as a reliable method of eliminating mistakes and of ensuring comprehension by the students. By having graduates join in this collective preparation, the Communists hope to make competent lecturers of them.

As a result of their rectification campaign, the Communists have discovered to their dismay that the earlier self-education campaign was not a complete success. The teachers are still clinging to some remnants of individuality. The Communists are now paying special attention to strengthening political and ideological education in the schools. The teachers, viewed by the Communists as engineers of the human soul, are being urged to continue voluntary self-education and self-remolding on the basis of the ideological remolding administered by the regime in the early days of the new government. The Communists claim that much has been achieved in ideological remolding among school teachers in the past, but they admit that the rectification campaign has proved that it is no easy matter for teachers to arm themselves with proletarian ideology, to take a firm stand amidst tempestuous class struggles, to distinguish clearly between right and wrong, and to guide the students along the right way.

Therefore, Premier Chou En-lai has decreed, the teachers should continue their efforts, learning Marxism and Leninism in order to acquire a correct political outlook, improving their attitude toward labor, and gradually making themselves one with the workers and peasants. Educational departments at all levels, and teachers, must now intensify the political and ideological education of the students in accordance with the ideological situation among the students. Teachers must train students as personnel for building up the country; they must train them to be loyal to the Socialist cause, to be plain-living and hard-working, and to combine mental and manual labor.

EDUCATION IN GRIM EARNEST

PEKING. If there should be riots or disturbances in this country they are to be viewed as the expression of different opinions rather than a threat to the government. This is the official view as enunciated publicly by Chou Yang, spokesman for the Communist party's central propaganda department. There was no admission by Mr. Chou that there have already been riots or disturbances. He was simply using the terms as an example of a further application of Chairman Mao's dictum, "let the flowers and the weeds bloom together." Mr. Chou did, however, refer to the possibility of demonstrations on the part of students with the suggestion that they had refused to attend classes. As he put it, "they are resorting to petitions or striking." He said the great majority of such incidents came about because of a bureaucratic attitude on the part of officialdom. The Communist policy now is: strive to overcome bureaucracy in all different branches and organizations, for if it develops it will encourage such disturbances. The people have freedom of speech and demonstration.

Again using the qualifying clause, "if there are riots and disturbances," Mr. Chou said he was sure they would be of a minor nature. The party assumes that the number of counter-revolutionaries in the country must be small, but it also feels that if any are involved in such disturbances their participation will be more easily detected if the incidents are dealt with correctly and if reasonable demands are met: "The relatively objective way of handling these situations is to allow different opinions to be expressed."

The rectification campaign gave the students an ideal opportunity to express their views of the path the Communists expected them to follow, but from the Communist point of view it must have seemed as if weeds instead of flowers were blooming. The reaction of the students to having their individualities channeled in a course set by the state was expressed in strikes, the throwing of a bomb at the Peking Medical College, and the organization at Peking University of a special club called the Hundred Flowers Society, which conducted an anti-Communist propaganda campaign. In the northwest, students of the Shensi Normal College in Sian put up posters opposing the Communist rule. A number of students demonstrated against the Red administration at Nanking University. The incident became so serious that the authorities had to call armed police.

The students would seem to be rebelling primarily against the mechanical, monotonous life which is their lot at college, although there is some indication they are beginning to doubt the sincerity and true intentions of the Communists, especially as they find that poverty, starvation, and ill health still prevail eight years after the Communist revolution. As long ago as October, 1956, the *Peking Daily* was complaining that many students, especially those in higher educational establishments, have been overburdened with classes. They have been living and studying in a state of excessive tension. A large proportion of China's students have to study sixty or seventy hours a week. Not only are they kept very busy through the day by their studies, but they have to work on Sundays and rest days as well. It would seem that the Communists are expecting them to be too industrious. The students are just not able to digest what they learn. Their minds are too tense. They have no chance of thinking and working by themselves, thinking and working along independent lines.

The Geological Institute at Changchun is a good example of the severity of the students' routine. There, the students have to stand up to eat. There are no stools, although the Institute, scoffingly referred to by even the Communist leaders as the "geological palace," is marked by the extravagance of a roof graced by 200,000 glazed tiles. Here is the daily routine of the Changchun students. They get up at 5:00 A.M. and have breakfast at 6:00 A.M. The first class starts at 7:00 A.M. At 9:00 A.M. there is a fifteen-minute break for physical exercise. Lunch is at noon and the school day ends at 5:00 P.M. A couple of evening hours are necessarily devoted to study, and most of the students go to bed at 9:00 P.M. This routine is followed six days a week. Sunday is a "day of rest" as are the half-dozen national holidays celebrated by the Communists. The students sleep six or eight to a room, the size of a single Toronto bedroom, provided rent free by the state; they get an allowance of 15½ yuan monthly ($6.20 Canadian) from the state out of which they pay 13½ yuan ($5.40) for food. Out of the balance they provide their own clothing and pay part of the cost of their books.

The effect of this routine on the students, and it applies all over China, is perhaps best expressed by Professor Hu Lun Tze, who spent three years studying at the University of Minnesota. He said efforts are now being made to reduce the work day for students. "Unless we do," he added, "I fear that the majority of our students will have a breakdown in their health."

The discontent among students is not confined to those who are studying at the universities. Stories are now appearing in

Chinese newspapers dealing with the refusal of graduates of primary and middle schools to go to work on farms while waiting admission to higher levels of education. This development highlights the dangers inherent in attempting to educate overnight a country of more than 600 million where for so many centuries the privilege of being able to read and write had been reserved for a relatively small group. When the Communist government launched its mass education campaign in 1949, it was faced with a national illiteracy rate of 80 per cent. In some areas it was 90 per cent. A further complication was the fact that some of the national minorities had no written language of their own. In setting out to make education available to all who wanted it, the Chinese Ministry of Education was handicapped by a lack of schools and teachers. These defects have compounded during the past year and explain why it is that thousands of students who have completed one level of education are unable to obtain admission to the next higher school. How many students are in this predicament is not known. The figures are not available but they present a problem that causes the authorities considerable concern. The dangers inherent in permitting a huge mass of students to lie about idle in the cities are obvious. Students must turn to farm work if they are unable to find a school to attend, for farm work offers the only possible outlet for their energies, and the need for help in the country is great. A list of foodstuffs is on the rationed list simply because agricultural production has not kept pace with increased population and purchasing power. China's industrial development has been rapid, but its factories cannot absorb any more workers, the supply of whom has been inflated by a flow of peasants to the cities. The population of Peking, for instance, has grown from 2 million to 4 million since 1949—an increase not entirely due to the fact that this city is now the national capital with the resulting influx of civil servants.

The development of China's education system over the past seven years has been rapid. Education is not compulsory—simply because there is a shortage of facilities. In 1956 there were 63 million children between the ages of seven and twelve attending primary school, or about 62 per cent of the total population in that age group. Middle school population (thirteen to eighteen) was 5 million, and there were 400,000 attending university. Since 1949, middle school attendance has increased about five times and primary students have more than doubled. Total school attendance in that year was 24 million. There are about a million children between the ages of three and seven in pre-school kindergartens.

In addition, the Education Ministry has established night schools for adult education where reading and writing are taught. About 4 million workers are now attending and 62 million farmers are taking instruction. About 20 million farmers have become literate since 1949.

Considerable attention has had to be given by the government to the age group of eighteen to forty from which it is drawing its chief support, not only ideologically but as a source of supply for the factories and for the armed services. About 200 million people in this group are illiterate, a condition the government is attempting to correct through special 400-hour courses.

OUT OF TUNE

PEKING. The current experiment of the Chinese government in permitting some degree of controversial discussion has taken one direction which is being heartily applauded by the more than 2,000 professional acting companies in this country. The Ministry of Culture has just announced that a directive lifting the present ban from twenty-six operas has been prepared and will go out shortly.

According to news reports, the main reasons for the ban, which was instituted after the Ministry had consulted with a number of leading opera actors, were that the operas were full of superstition, feudal morality, sex, murder, and incitement against national minorities. One report added: "These operas were banned between 1950 and 1952, during the land reform and other political activities. . . . Now with actors no longer catering to low tastes as in the Kuomintang days (before 1949) and the better appreciative ability of audiences, there is little danger of public taste being corrupted." To complete the circle we have this explanation of a Ministry spokesman: "In the competition between good and bad operas, more and more better operas will be produced. Evaluation and criticism of operas in discussions and the press will encourage good operas. It will be better to allow the free play of controversy to settle such questions rather than banning by administrative action."

Although they are not officially credited with having had an effect, there is no doubt that public apathy and passive resistance to new operas and plays which had as their theme modern political lectures, have forced the government to have a second thought on the banning of certain operas. Unfortunately for China's 150,000 actors, the official ban on a small number of plays, coupled with the widely publicized urging of the Ministry of Culture that the popular element in the traditional heritage should be sought and stressed, and that backward and unhealthy elements in it should be criticized, meant that thousands of historic plays ceased to be presented for fear the producers and actors would be risking a charge of failing to be positive in their thinking.

The possibility of a renaissance in Chinese opera seems to have had its origin in what was, for the China of today, a daring experiment by the Peking Opera Company early this year. The company revived a historical favorite called *Yang Sse-lang Revisits His Mother*. The opera, which affords great dramatic opportunities to the actor, and has fast movement, fine characterization, and stirring music, had not been presented since the conclusion of the armed revolution in 1949. It had not been officially banned. It had been dropped from the repertory because it tells the story of a general taken prisoner in battle, who came to terms with his captors and married the daughter of the enemy king. After a time the general felt a longing to visit his home. With the help of his wife, he crossed over to pay his mother a sorrowful visit—but insisted on returning afterwards. In China's mood of the early post-revolution years, the opera's theme was out of tune. It could perhaps be viewed as making a sympathetic figure of a man who was a traitor to his country, but it was assumed audiences did not want to go to it—and actors stifled the desire to perform it.

This opera and the heated public discussion which followed its revival have apparently had the end result of a general easing of government restrictions on the themes of operas and plays. Many critics, dramatists, and actors continued to feel that the elevation of personal sentiment above national honor was harmful propaganda. Others considered that the opera, because of its artistic merit, deserved presentation again. One critic wrote: "We must not underestimate our audiences. There is no need to worry that they will all become traitors after attending such a performance. On the contrary, the public can give us a lot of guidance in reviving the old dramas and preserving our national tradition." The public gave its answer in packed houses for *Yang Sse-lang*, a positive reaction against a steady diet of politically correct entertainment which limited the available plays to about half a dozen which were presented and re-presented in monotonous succession throughout the country.

In the soul-searching that has gone on in Chinese theatrical circles in recent months, it was concluded that few plays were being brought out because of a lack of understanding in applying the policy of theater reform. Drama workers, critics, and the cultural committees of local governments all had somehow acquired the idea that the theater must be a place of education for the people. It was now being publicly said that their standard of what was educational was too narrow.

Many of these guardians of public thinking tended to measure plays solely by political standards, ignoring both historical context and aesthetic considerations and sometimes substituting personal likes and dislikes for objective critical judgment. Present-day social morality (as defined by the Communists) was used as a yardstick for changing or shelving historical plots or characters. Plays that showed a man with two wives (a common thing in China for centuries) were condemned as not in accordance with the new marriage law. Some even suggested that tragedy should not be played because it does not reflect the people's optimistic spirit. There were cases in which actors stopped playing some of their favorite roles because they doubted if their characters were positive by the new standards. Others introduced modern slogans into the mouths of historical characters. White-nosed clowns were taboo because some people declared that to paint the nose white is an insult to the laboring people. Ghosts were frowned off the stage, due to a failure to distinguish between mythology and superstition.

The decision to relax restrictions on operas and plays undoubtedly stems directly from a two-week conference, called by the operatic drama department of the Ministry of Culture last June, at which the whole problem of rediscovery was discussed. There the harm done by dogmatic attitudes was apparently frankly faced. It was agreed there had been mistakes, that a good play need have no obvious message, and that there should be no obstacle to audiences seeing dramas they liked and drawing their own conclusions from them.

Proof of this was found in public acceptance of the controversial *Story of the Lute*, a 600-year-old play familiar to all Chinese theater lovers. The play tells of Chao Wu-niang, a deserted wife who ate husks so that her husband's parents could have rice, and sold her hair to give them a proper burial when they died. Finally she made a long and difficult journey to find her husband, a scholar who had won first place in a civil examination and had been forced to marry the prime minister's daughter. There was considerable dispute as to whether this play upheld or condemned feudal morality. Some members of the Hunan Provincial Drama Company, for instance, thought the trouble was in the ending—in which the husband retained both wives. They reintroduced a variation which had once existed in this old tale, in which the wife was trampled to death by her husband's horse while he himself was struck by lightning. The audiences rebelled at this by, as one critic put it, "voting with their feet." They stayed away from the theater. The company reverted to the former finale, seeing reason in the argument of the theatergoers that, in the circumstances of the time, the husband could have behaved in no other way and that the wife showed extraordinary courage and loyalty. So, the *Lute* is again being staged in its original version and thousands of people enjoy a good weep at the sufferings of the heroine and rejoice at the happy ending.

And now many older artists are digging into their trunks for scripts of plays in which they once took roles. The Ministry is doing its part by exempting all operatic drama companies from entertainment tax and allocating 5 million yuan ($2 million Canadian) to assist theatrical companies and individual artists who have financial troubles.

SUMMER PALACE ON SUNDAY

PEKING. There are about 4 million people in this capital city of China and about a million go on Sundays to tour the grounds of the Summer Palace. At least, that's the way it appears to the tourist who heeds the advice of a friend, now many thousands of miles away, that Sunday is the best day of the week to visit the historic spot. It is open on all the other days of the week, but Sunday is the only day on which most people of Peking have the necessary time (a minimum of about twelve hours is required for bare coverage of the high spots) to thoroughly investigate this former vacation playground of the feudal emperors of the Sung dynasty.

So it was that, accompanied by Mr. Yen, my interpreter, I elbowed my way for about eight foot-weary hours through a solid mass of Chinese men, women, and children, broken here and there by small groups of other foreigners looking just as weary as I, but seemingly just as determined to personally sample the magnificence of the Summer Palace, which is described by the Chinese as a conglomeration of the excellence of all China's famous scenic resorts. Perhaps from the Canadian point of view, the palace, the Chinese name of which is Yi Ho Yuan, is best described as containing a little bit of such landmarks as a museum, a city park, an amusement park, and a beach on the Great Lakes, all rolled into one. Here, within 823 acres, four-fifths of which are lake, there are more than a hundred buildings—halls, towers, pavilions, bridges, and pagodas, each making its own contribution in history, scenery, amusement, or just plain loafing in the sun and fresh air.

Here is the repository of some of China's past, some of it grand because it can now be enjoyed by millions at the cost of a few cents admission; some of it not so grand when the cost in man hours it took to create it is counted. The Summer Palace had its beginning early in the twelfth century when the leaders of the Kingdom of Chin, residents of a more tropical portion of China, sought an alternative palace for the summer months. While anxious to escape the summer heat of the south, the royal travelers were reluctant to part with the scenery to which they had become accustomed, so the Summer Palace and its grounds are the result of an attempt eight centuries ago to recreate in the cooler north the familiar surroundings of the permanent residence in south China. The result can only be described as a masterpiece of artificial landscaping in a skillful blending of woods, water, hills, and architecture. It is impossible to guess where nature begins and man ends in his deliberate imitation of the wonders of hills and gardens famous in other parts of this widespread nation.

The Summer Palace actually has had two lives. The original palace, known as Yuan Ming Yuan, was burned down during the Taiping revolution against high taxation imposed by the Manchu government. The present palace, west of the ruins of Yuan Ming Yuan, was built by the Manchu Empress Dowager Tzu Hsi, the last of China's monarchs with the exception of Pu Yi, who abdicated in 1912. (Pu Yi had a brief return engagement when he was made puppet emperor of Manchuria by the Japanese in the 1930's. He is now in jail in northeast China.) The Dowager Empress' efforts in rebuilding the Summer Palace are mainly recalled today by the famous Marble

Boat (sometimes known as Stone Boat), a land-locked replica of a canal barge built by the Empress with funds which had been collected to train a naval force for China.

There is only one entrance (also the exit) to the Summer Palace, a narrow one, known as the East Palace Gate, and as is to be expected the crush is considerable, comparable perhaps to a subway in the rush hour. How the thousands of families reach the palace is something of a mystery, for the modern four-lane highway which leads to it from central Peking was not crowded with buses or cars nor were there many vehicles parked in the ample space provided for that purpose just a few steps away from the entrance. But come they do, with their picnic baskets and their vacuum jugs of hot water for the delightfully mild green tea which all Chinese drink at any given opportunity. For those who wanted them there were available various soft drinks, warm beer, and something resembling a popsicle, the flavor of which still remains a mystery. Not to be overlooked in the equipment necessary for the day's outing is the camera. If there were a million people at the Summer Palace that Sunday then there must have been 100,000 cameras. Every little group had its camera, of various vintages, and all were snapping family shots.

It is impossible to describe the Summer Palace in one breath and it is equally impossible to absorb its beauties in one visit, even if there weren't another million persons attempting to do the same thing. Briefly, as you go along the road to the palace, you see Wan Shou Shan (Longevity Hill), Fu Hsiang Ko (Pavilion of the Fragrance of God) and the towering pagoda on the top of the Jade Spring Hill. The one-fifth of the grounds which is solid consists of man-made hillocks which provide a base for the four parts into which the park is divided —the erstwhile imperial living quarters and the court buildings, the spectacular architectural design leading up to Chih Hui Hai (Sea of Wisdom Temple) on the highest point, the

61

ruins of the old palace, and the landscaped stream at the back of the hill.

Immediately on entering the east palace gate there are three groups of buildings approached through courtyards—Lo Shou Tang (Hall of Delight in Longevity), Teh Ho Yuan (Hall of Virtuous Harmony), the old Empress' theater and stage, and Jen Shou Tien (Hall of Benevolence and Longevity). This and the Hall of Delight in Longevity are now used for exhibitions and the Hall of Virtuous Harmony is a rest home for workers. Connecting the buildings and the courts all along the shore of Kunming Lake are a series of covered promenades, richly painted. The paintings are scenes at the Summer Palace itself.

One of the more scenic portions of the grounds is Hsieh Chu Yuan (Garden of Harmonious Interest). Here pink lotus glows in the pond, wistaria casts its purple blossoms over pavilions standing over the water, and bamboos wave among artistically grouped rocks. This is a typical Chinese landscape painting come to life. It is modeled after the scenery of the Chi Chang Garden on Hui Hill in Wusih, Kiangsu province. The Seventeen Arch Bridge is one of six bridges which, together with an embankment, are copied from a famous beauty spot by the West Lake in Hangchow. Here, too, is strengthened the resolve that the Summer Palace must be seen again but only on a day when the rest of Peking is at work.

BIRTH CONTROL

PEKING. The Chinese government is now prepared to concede that drastic measures are required if this country's teeming population is to be kept under control. The government, it is reported, has agreed to legalize sterilization and abortion, both of which have until now been strictly controlled by law. Erasing of restrictions on sterilization and abortion is planned as a supplement to the widely publicized campaign to persuade married couples to practise their own birth control through the use of contraceptives. It is on the widest possible distribution of contraceptives and of the knowledge of their use that the government has pinned its hope of success in the planned parenthood campaign promoted by the Communist party in the fear that the increasing population would swamp the government's five-year industrial expansion plans.

Industrialization has resulted in a sharp increase in China's population as it has in every other country, but perhaps nowhere else in the world is the problem of population as pressing as it is here. The decision to resort to legal sterilization and abortion is viewed here as a reluctant admission by the Communists that China's teeming millions present an internal problem of huge magnitude; one which must of necessity be considered first in assessing the multitude of problems which arise in the transition from an almost wholly agricultural economy to a semi-industrialized state.

It is easy to understand the regime's reluctance to finally admit that China's rapidly increasing population has to be stabilized by some means, however drastic. In so doing, the government, as it has in the past, has chosen to ignore the pure Marxist doctrine that the more people there are the better. In China's case that is proving not to be the case, and some of the troubles the government now finds itself in are a direct result of the application to China of Marxist theory, since, until recently, the Communist party openly encouraged people to have more babies.

It is understood that under the new regulations now being prepared, the sterilization operation will be provided at public expense, at the request of a man and wife, provided both agree. The government is not prepared to suggest which person should be sterilized but hopes it will be the husband, since the operation is simpler and less expensive. It will not be performed unless a medical board is satisfied the couple completely understand that they can no longer have children. Abortions will be available, also at public expense, at the request of the wife only, provided that she is in good health, has not had an abortion in the previous twelve months, and is not more than three months pregnant. Again approval must be given by a medical board.

If the campaign to control births through the use of contraceptives has failed, and the legalizing of sterilization and abortion would seem to indicate this, it certainly cannot have failed because of a lack of enthusiasm and ingenuity on the part of those charged with popularizing it. There are thousands of mobile birth control units wandering the countryside, and all larger cities and towns have permanent birth control centers where staffs of doctors and nurses daily conduct thousands of men and women, most of them young, through a frank demonstration of what is accomplished through the use of contraceptives.

There is one of these displays in Peihai Park where, at the beginning of the tenth century, Emperor Tai Tsung of the Liao Kingdom had his villa. In the twelfth century the Golden Tartars dredged lakes and the excavated earth was used to build Chiunghuatao (Islet of Treasure) on which hillocks and palaces were erected in a plan to reproduce what was visualized as a fairyland. It would be reasonable to assume that the emperor, with the high regard for children that is traditional with the Chinese, would surely turn in his grave at the use to which part of his fairyland is being devoted. His embarrassment would be no less than that of this Westerner suddenly brought face to face with the inner details of male and female

ABOVE. Teahouse and pavilion in grounds of Summer Palace, Peking, where standing room only is the rule, especially on Sundays. BELOW. Entrance to Summer Palace guarded by a lion which provides favorite perch for those having their pictures taken.

LEFT. Street peddler pauses on Chungking street. She is selling apples and chestnuts and when she finds a good spot will use the stool and the scales in the basket at left.

Last of the capitalists. Pedicab owners in Peking still operate as free agents but when the transition to Communism is completed they will be workers in a completely publicly owned economy. This stage has been reached by pedicab operators in Wuhan who are organized in a co-operative which owns the pedicabs.

Youthful participant in parade at Changchun. Occasion was June 1, a school holiday, and thousands of young people paraded to the People's Park where they played community games. This young fellow was in a pageant arranged by the teachers to celebrate the date which is known in the Communist world as International Children's Day.

A typical baby carriage made from bamboo. Big sister is tired of pushing little brother and climbs in for a rest.

Pedicab operator in Peking.

BELOW. Huge loads are transported in Red China on these commercial versions of the pedicab. This is Morrison Street in Peking which has 100,000 of these vehicles. Behind it are a few samples of the 50,000 bicycles used in the capital city.

RIGHT. Scene on Pearl River
at Canton.

BELOW. Porters struggling to
pull a heavily laden cart
through the streets of Chungking where everything is
moved by humans because the
city is so hilly donkeys and
ponies cannot operate.

LEFT. Freight boat on Yangtze, propelled by manpower. On difficult upriver trip, crew get out on shore and pull boat with ropes.

OPPOSITE TOP. A houseboat on the Yangtze River. Boat floats down the river, without power, requiring only steering by its crew. On return trip it is towed by a tug, along with several others. BOTTOM. Famous marble boat in Summer Palace, Peking, built by the Dowager Empress Tzu Hsi with funds collected for the Chinese navy.

LEFT. Cliffside road in Yangtze valley, used as tow-path for hauling boats up river.

TOP. Chinese mother and child at Shumchun station, entry point from Kowloon into Red China. BOTTOM. Billboard poster advertisement for a Chinese "comic book" which features, among other things, a series on American Imperialism.

reproductive organs sketched in bold relief on the wall of the Pi Yun (birth control) center.

Perhaps the campaign to popularize birth control through contraceptives has boomeranged in that the simplicity of the method has been over-emphasized to the point where the population is viewing even the simplest devices as too complicated. This was revealed by Dr. Hwong Chin Wen, director of the maternal health department, who threw her arms in the air and observed: "Now the women want a contraceptive they can take by mouth, or by a shot in the arm." While admitting that the country's scientists are investigating reports that Chinese country doctors (herbalists) have developed an oral contraceptive, Dr. Hwong declared: "Although we agree science should serve the interests of the people, we draw the line at making birth control too easy." It would seem, however, that it cannot be made too easy if China is not to bulge at the seams in a few years with too many people.

A Chinese professor has publicly estimated that the ideal population for China with its known resources and agricultural possibilities is 800 million. Chinese economists who scoff at this as being simply one man's opinion do, at the same time, express some concern, since population threatens to outstrip the country's ability to grow enough food. What they cannot ignore is the country's present population and the rate at which it is increasing. It is conservatively estimated that there are 650 million people in China proper today. This does not include Formosa where there are about 10 million. The annual birth rate is about 30 million and the death rate 13 million so that every year China's population increases by 17 million. This means that each year the population of Canada is added to China's millions. At this rate of increase the ideal population of 800 million will be reached by 1966 but most likely sooner, since an increase in public health measures is gradually reducing infant mortality and the diseases which tended, through natural deaths, to more or less balance China's population in the past.

It is extremely doubtful if the government will resort to compulsion to encourage sterilization and abortion. Not even a government which feels it is as solidly entrenched as does China's government is likely to risk the wrath of a population which, by tradition, is opposed to birth control—a tradition in which there still persists the desire for descendants, particularly sons. And in popularizing its new approach to birth control, the government will, in the words of one economist, discover that its toughest task will be to convince the Chinese male, particularly the peasant, that the act of sterilization won't make him impotent.

CAN CHINA GROW ENOUGH FOOD?

PEKING. The most vital question in China today is whether this country can grow enough food to feed her rapidly increasing population and to export in return for needed industrial equipment. The answer to this question is the key to China's industrial advancement. To acquire the equipment essential for building an industrial structure, China has one main source of foreign credit—her exports of foodstuffs. If, as has happened in the past (as recently as 1956), there is a poor crop, then China's industrialization falters, or else is maintained only by snatching the very food from out of the mouths of her people, about two-thirds of whom are solely engaged in producing that food.

There are those outside China (and inside) who are skeptical of her ability to accomplish her dual task. It has been estimated by a U.S. technologist that it is impossible for China to keep up the average household consumption of food and at the same time provide the necessary non-food crops and agricultural exports. China, he pointed out, was not able to increase her agricultural production by 13 per cent between 1952 and 1957, his own calculation of the minimum increase required to keep China's new industrial wheels rolling. This outsider's view is, of course, repudiated by the Chinese. It is admitted by L. K. Yung, research director for the state planning commission, that the average producing level of foodstuffs in China is still very low. At the same time, the annual increase since 1952 has been about 5 per cent, as opposed to a population increase of 2 per cent. This, Mr. Yung insisted, is evidence that China is continuing to feed her population.

The question arises at this time because of an announcement in Rangoon that China has signed a contract to purchase 50,000 tons of Burmese rice. Rice is one of the commodities rationed in China. The others are cotton, flour, and edible oils (generally peanut oil). Yet China is exporting these rationed agricultural products in exchange for the produce required to maintain her industrial growth. For instance, she has a trade agreement with Ceylon under which China has undertaken to ship 270,000 tons of rice in exchange for 50,000 tons of Ceylonese rubber annually. Another trade agreement which expired last year was for the annual exchange of 150,000 tons of Burmese rice for Chinese export commodities of equal value. The announcement that China will get 50,000 tons of rice from Burma this year was carried in the local newspapers. It said only that it was a contract to purchase; there was no suggestion that the deal was on an exchange of goods basis.

Another problem now facing the state planning commission, whose activities intimately affect the lives of every one of China's 650 million people, is how to supply the raw materials needed for export when three-quarters of this country's exports are agricultural products. Seeking the answer to this question took me to Tsao Hsiao Chi, an engineer of the department of agricultural and reclamation planning bureau. Mr. Tsao is a gentleman who deals in big things: masses of people and huge chunks of land. On the one hand, he is concerned with the organization of state collective farms and the process of ideological remolding which convinces the peasants that it is to their advantage to cast their lot with the co-operatives. The latest estimate (exact figures are seldom obtainable from Chinese government officials) is that more than 90 per cent of the peasants (representing 110 million households) are now working in co-operatives. Since it is also estimated that 230 million Chinese are now eating food not grown by themselves or by members of their families, it can be concluded that about 360 million peasants have responded to the urging to throw their lot in with the co-operatives. It is likely that most of the balance of about 40 million peasants are located in areas where it has not yet been practical to insist on the mutual-aid and co-operative movement.

In northeast China, there are vast state-controlled farms. One of these state farms contains 40,000 mou (about 6,600 acres) and provides an excellent illustration of how mechanization reduces the need for manpower. About 1,000 men are required to operate the state farm as against an estimated 10,000 if cultivation and harvesting depended upon the preponderance of men, as is still the case in most of the arable areas of China.

Co-operative farming is one phase of what Mr. Tsao describes as land reclamation. The other is reclaiming the so-called barren lands—barren in the sense that except for fitful cultivation by nomad tribes the land has been used only for pasture. The farms in these new areas are state farms controlled by the Ministry of Agriculture. So it is that the Mongolian steppes are growing wheat and soyabeans to help feed China's millions of mouths. In Sinkiang province in the northwest, once idle land is growing cotton. The land is dry there, and it has been necessary first to wash the earth since it has a high alkaline content. This has been accomplished by tiling to lower the existing water table and then flushing the area with irrigated water. (In South China the cotton yield has been doubled by using this method.) In the same way China is developing new cotton-growing areas in the salt lands of the Yangtze Valley, and along the East Sen and Po rivers in Hopei and Shantung provinces.

Since most of the new farm area was sparsely settled before the present activity began, the natural question is "where did the manpower come from to work the land?" Mr. Tsao had a ready and simple answer. In Sinkiang, China is putting to work some of the many millions of men she has in uniform— the army is working the land. Where soldiers are not available, manpower is requisitioned from other areas. Mr. Tsao hastened to add that in this instance the word requisition is not as menacing as it would appear to be. "We simply say we need so many men and our request is filled by volunteers," he explained.

Flood control measures, increased irrigation, and reform of local farm methods are also doing much to help China feed herself. Kweichow province is perhaps a good illustration of the value of reformed farming. This province had always been a buyer of foodstuffs until 1954–5 when it shipped out 250,000 tons of grain for the first time in its history. Much of this was due to reform of the local farm methods which had been extremely backward.

It is expected this year to put to work more than 2 million acres of new land, and China now estimates that at the end of 1962, accounting for the increase in population, there will be a per capita production of 830 pounds of grain as against 704 pounds in 1956.

THE GOOD HOUSEWIFE CAMPAIGN

SHENYANG. Northeast China, of which this city (which is known to foreigners as Mukden) is the chief metropolis, has long played a historic role in China. From here came the Manchus who were to rule China from 1368 until the throne toppled in the Sun Yat-sen revolution of 1912. It was here, too, that the Japanese made their first real penetration into China, when they occupied this city in 1931 preparatory to their attempt to conquer the whole country. And it was from here that the Japanese were finally dislodged in 1945 by the Russians. The Russians gave way some months later to Chiang Kai-shek's Kuomintang army, 100,000 members of which were beseiged in this city by the Communists in 1948 and laid down their arms without firing a shot when faced with the alternative of being starved into submission.

Shenyang is also the nerve center of China's chief industrial area, for despite the government's efforts to disperse its industrial base, almost 70 per cent of industry is still located in the north and northeast. It is only natural, then, that a movement involving China's so recently emancipated women should start from this factory area and sweep the country. The movement is the Wu-hao, the five essentials of the role of women in Socialist construction.

There is an old Chinese proverb which says: "A tree has its roots, water its source, and everything its start." And so, here is the story of the Wu-hao, or Good Housewife Campaign, and how it affects the daily lives of the Chinese. The Wu-hao had their birth, after the passing of the Marriage Law in 1950, in the sudden awareness of the Chinese housewives that they were the equal of their husbands in all respects. With this new equality came the realization that housewives also had some added responsibilities, one of which was to familiarize themselves with what went on in the factories where their husbands worked. The greatest problem was their failure to adapt their household work to these conditions, to realize that industry is run by the clock, that factory work demands regularity of its workers.

Self-criticism in this country is almost a national phobia, so it is not strange that the housewives of northeast China concluded they weren't considerate enough of their husbands. They often failed to prepare meals on time. Others bickered with their neighbors and quarreled with their husbands. The wives realized that under these circumstances their husbands could not get sufficient rest after returning home from the factory and, what is most important in a nation dedicated to the principle that all should labor, these home disturbances impaired the health of their husbands and indirectly affected their work. There was also the point that when the wives were confined, or when they or their dependents became ill, the workers were immediately in trouble because there was no one to look after things, thus taking up time with home affairs which should have been spent at benches or lathes.

Because of the advanced industrialization of northeast China, the wives of that area had a better understanding of the problems and so they got together. Proposals were put forward that a good housewife should excel in three things. Others suggested five. At last, five essentials were agreed on and these became the Wu-hao, now the subject of a country-wide propaganda effort. They have been adopted by the All-China Democratic Women's Federation and the All-China Federation of Trade Unions. These organizations have called upon wives of workers and housewives throughout China to set afoot the Wu-hao, to help in China's Socialist construction.

Based on the original proposals of the wives of northeast China, the Wu-hao (five essentials) were clarified as follows: Arrange your home life in a proper way; help and unite with your neighbors; encourage your husband to work and study well; educate your children in the right way; study hard yourself.

As explained in the propaganda campaign designed to popularize the Wu-hao in the rest of China, the first point means the establishment of a new home life in which a spirit of mutual respect, love, and help, of harmony and solidarity prevails. Money should be spent in a planned way and frugality cherished as a virtue.

The second point means maintaining amicable relations with neighbors. Housewives should have a deep regard for and help one another. In safeguarding public welfare, they should educate and encourage one another.

The third point means that the housewives should, with the interest of the national construction in mind, prevail upon their husbands to work and study hard in a common endeavor to keep pace with the times.

The fourth point means that housewives should educate their children in the spirit of Socialism. The parents should set themselves as examples for their children to follow so that the new generation may grow up under their tender care, sound in mind as well as in body.

The fifth point means that the housewives should learn to read and write, acquaint themselves with the policies of the state in particular and politics in general, improve their understanding, and acquire new knowledge.

During the past year the five essentials have been widely publicized in more than a hundred cities and have been credited with being responsible for nine workers getting awards for meritorious service and one being elected as an advanced worker, because, since they were free from worries at home, they were very keen on their jobs. The badge of merit, with its red star in the center of a white and gold background, is much coveted in this country which has not yet adopted the cash bonus reward system for instances of outstanding work.

Obviously there now arises the question of whether the Wu-hao tend to restrict women to the confines of their homes and to deprive them of their chance of working in society. The authorities say this is not so. "In new China where the people have taken the state power securely in their hands, women are placed on an equal footing with men. But women cannot be considered fully emancipated if they do not take up some outside employment," it is explained. Government policy is still that housewives must increasingly take part in political activity and community work. The Wu-hao do not in any way confine them to their homes. By making a good job of their supplementary role in the national construction, housewives earn the respect of the people and consequently raise their status in society.

Since there is equality of pay for work done in China, women are turning increasingly to outside jobs, and for a testimonial to the effectiveness of the Wu-hao, here is the brief story of Kuan Ching-nien, a peasant woman in Hunan: "Now I've earned my own work points and can support myself. I'm in every way my husband's equal." Mrs. Kuan concluded by explaining that formerly her husband used to beat her, cursing her for having lived on him. Now he has a talk with her before spending on anything and the couple get on well together.

RINGING A CHANGE

SHENYANG. Whether the principle involved is that two bells are better than one is not known, but it is a fact that the made-in-China alarm clock, the article most frequently and proudly displayed for sale in this country's shops, is equipped with two huge bells. These proudly provide the base for a carrying handle which would effectively serve a brief case. The most popular and most reliable alarm clock sells for about $6 Canadian and for most factory workers it represents an invest-ment of about a fifth of a month's pay. It will be readily realized, therefore, that the acquisition of an alarm clock is not the result of a snap decision; nevertheless, since most of China's industrial workers get up with the sun in order to get in an hour or so of schooling before reporting for work at 7:00 A.M., an alarm clock would seem to be a necessity.

It is for this reason that I am passing on the story of a clock as it affected Chao Ying-chi, a young worker in a machine tool factory in this northeast China industrial center. For the facts I am indebted to Kao Shen, writer for a Chinese women's magazine.

Ying-chi was an undisciplined young worker. Every morn-ing, when everyone else was heading to work in high spirits, Ying-chi was still under the quilt. He was notorious for being late; for leaving before his shift ended; and even for being away from work without good reason. That was why more than once he had been severely criticized by his workmates. When his wife, Lo Min, chided him he would invariably say it was all because they didn't have a timepiece. But whenever she proposed that they buy a clock, he never lacked reasons why they should do something else. The couple had been married about a year. Lo Min decided to save bit by bit from the family budget until there was enough money to buy the clock. All this she did without Ying-chi's knowledge, con-soling herself with the thought that, once they had a clock, he would get up in time and would never again be late for work.

One day, Ying-chi saw before his eyes a new, shiny, alarm clock on the table. He quickly realized what Lo Min had done and was moved by her thoughtfulness. He examined the clock carefully, listening to the tick and trying the alarm. "Fine,

fine!" he exclaimed. "Now that we've got a clock, I'll never be late again, on my word of honor!" Ying-chi kept his word. The next morning he got up without being urged, and got to work at 7:00 A.M. for the first time since he had got married.

A few days later, however, Ying-chi was back into his old habits. Each morning after the alarm had gone off, he would look at the clock a dozen times, and wait in bed until the last possible second. Lo Min thought of another way to get round his laziness. She set the clock half an hour ahead. He was just on time, though he thought he was late as usual. When Ying-chi got to know the secret many days later, he found, somewhat to his surprise, that he had acquired the early habit.

But something had long been at the back of Lo Min's mind —Ying-chi was not yet an advanced worker. Whenever she mentioned this to him, he brushed the subject aside, irritably. One day they were at it again; Ying-chi was so enraged that he went to bed without supper. Later that night, love for her husband getting the better of her exasperation, Lo Min poured out her heart to him. "I love you and expect much of you. But, you've got to know that it isn't a bigger wage envelope I want from you, but that you'll make something of your job. People don't think well of you; they say you're interested only in dancing. Each time I hear this I feel ashamed. I'm sure you would feel the same if you heard somebody talking about me that way. But despite all the gossip, I have faith in you. I know you'll make good. Before we got married, nobody cared for you, and it was easy for you to go on the loose. But it's different now; you've got a home of your own. Besides, you're a father. You ought to feel a little more responsible. Others can make their mark and there isn't any reason why you can't do so."

There were tears in Ying-chi's eyes. The words tugged at his heart. He didn't say anything but clasped Lo Min's hands. Next day, Ying-chi was home earlier than usual. The moment he entered the room he said to Lo Min: "Lo Min, see if I can't win an advanced worker title!" There was a confident smile on the face that was so dear to her. She looked at him with mixed feelings. "I'm serious," he added, as if fearing she would not believe him. "I had a talk with the party (Communist party) branch secretary this afternoon. He didn't lecture me, but everything he said was so convincing that I think he must be right."

In April last year, Ying-chi was cited as an advanced worker in his own shop, and now he is listed among the advanced workers of the whole factory. So Lo Min smiles happily and her face flushes with just pride as she thinks of all that has happened since she first decided to buy the alarm clock that is merrily ticking on the side table.

TIMBER MINISTER IN TROUBLE

PINKIANG (HARBIN). Not far from here as distances go in this country, which is almost the size of Canada, China is conducting its first scientific program of utilizing forests. The program, based on a recently completed survey and classification of resources, is being conducted in the Changpaishan Mountains, near the Chinese-Korean border. The program lays down plans for felling trees, for improving conditions for the growth of trees, and for the regeneration of the forests. The same type of program is being instituted in other areas. In the Greater and Lesser Khingan Mountains, also in this part of China, to the north, 50 million acres of forest have been surveyed and photographed from the air. At the opposite end of the country, in Tibet and western Szechuan province, great forests of spruce, fir, and Chinese hemlock-spruce have been surveyed. Many of these trees, which provide excellent construction lumber, are 200 or 300 years old. The survey parties are mapping areas for conservation as well as for lumbering.

More than 5,000 kinds of trees and other woody plants grow in China, more kinds than in any other country in the world. They range from the deciduous pine in the frozen mountain ranges of this northeast area to the betel and coconut on torrid Hainan Island. Some trees that still grow in China have no counterpart in any other country. Among these are the 3,000-year-old Giant of Arisan, a type of red cedar, and the Metasequoia, an early predecessor of the huge California Redwood and now extinct outside China.

The fact is, however, that only 5 per cent of China is wooded, and her reserves of timber are so low that a special minister has been put in charge of all timber that is cut. He is Lo Lung-chi, and my interview with him took place in his home. Unfortunately for the ostensible subject to be explored —forests—the interview devolved into a lengthy discussion of Communism and what has happened to China since the end of the revolution in 1949. However, I was able to find out from him why there is such a shortage of timber in China. This, according to Mr. Lo, is a legacy of the past when, he said, timber was felled without any attempt at replacement. Generations of peasants, driven from their farms for a variety of reasons, burned the trees off hillsides to reclaim new fields. This constant deforestation, Mr. Lo explained, contributed to the vicious circle of natural disasters—flood, drought, and the impoverishment of the soil. Moreover, it is claimed that the Japanese, during their fourteen years' occupation of this area, cut down more than 131 million cubic yards of lumber and did not plant any new trees. The Kuomintang, the present regime's predecessor as China's government, is accused of having felled a tremendous quantity of timber in Szechuan province and then to have left the logs to rot for lack of transport.

So that explains why Mr. Lo, virtual dictator of timber resources, almost counts each piece individually. Before he can cut a tree he must secure the permission of the Ministry of Forestry and then only on the basis of an estimate of needs which is prepared at the beginning of each year. The needs of the entire country, including local lumberyards in cities and towns and the peasants who use wood for fuel, must be projected a year ahead, and, wherever possible, cement, steel, and bamboo (of which there is plenty in China) are substituted by government direction. "At the beginning of each year," Mr. Lo said, "we must know how many buildings are going to be constructed (of all types), how many railway ties will be needed. We even must know the number of props required by our mines."

An over-all plan for the protection, effective management, and scientific use of forest resources began to take shape in 1950. The first step was a propaganda campaign through newspaper articles, cartoons, lectures, posters, and even plays, to emphasize the need for preserving and protecting the forests. Through local government bodies, fire prevention and firefighting organizations were set up and equipment was provided. Villages were linked by warning systems, and volunteer patrols were formed to watch for fires during the dangerous seasons when it was hot, dry, and windy. The common practice of setting fire to scrub or weeds when reclaiming land was prohibited wherever it might endanger forests. In northeast China alone, according to a recent report of the Ministry of Forestry, more than 2,000 miles of fire lanes were cleared around the edges of forests, and along railway lines where sparks from passing trains caused about 30 per cent of China's forest fires. This area is reported to have more than 200 forest watchtowers and its firefighting network has telephone lines stretching for 620 miles. Both here and in Inner Mongolia, aircraft patrols supplement observation from the ground.

To protect natural new growth, many hilly areas have been made into preserves. Access to them for gathering firewood or grazing is strictly regulated. Government regulations also limit the proportion of trees which may be cut down in felling areas. Under a new system introduced in 1955 the timber stands are marked out into strips and only alternate ones may be felled.

Large-scale reforestation projects are under way, not only to provide materials for construction and industry, but to help control the natural calamities which plague this country. Big shelter belts, known as China's Great Wall of Trees, are being planted. The program is designed to protect nearly 52 million acres of land, including cultivated areas and sandy wastes. Between 1950 and 1955 more than 12½ million acres were reforested and, in the spring of 1956, 9 million acres of trees, an area as large as Belgium, were set out. A shelter belt now being planted from eastern Inner Mongolia into these northeast provinces will be the biggest in Asia when it is completed in 1967. Nearly 700 miles long and 180 miles wide, it is designed to transform 42 million acres of wind-blown steppes into fertile field and pasture. Other belts are located along the North China coast in the provinces of Shantung, Hopei, and Kiangsu, and in the northeast to protect cultivated land from gales that blow in from the sea.

In southern China, with its warm climate and abundant rainfall, the aim of the large-scale tree planting now being carried on is to develop useful timber, and supplies of raw materials such as tung oil, resins, camphor, rubber, lacquer, cork, and tannin.

When I spoke to Mr. Lo I was well aware of his past political history. He is one of the few non-Communist members of the government, a representative of one of the various political parties which enable the Communists to maintain the farce that China is ruled by a government consisting of all parties. The supreme organ of state power is ostensibly the

National People's Congress, consisting of members drawn from the nine political parties now presumably existing in the country. There are 1,226 deputies to the Congress and 269 of these come from eight of the parties. The Communist party has the rest. The party to which Mr. Lo belongs is the China Democratic League, of which he is a vice-president. The League sends 82 deputies to the People's Congress and represents the next largest group to that controlled by the Communists. The League was organized in 1941 to participate in the war against Japan, and later was outlawed by the Kuomintang regime when General Marshall and other United States mediators suggested that the League might be able to form a government, since it was impossible to get the Communists and the Kuomintang to agree on a coalition. The League's members were given some rough treatment by the Kuomintang government for their willingness to supplant it after attempts at mediation had failed and Marshall had left the country. It is not surprising, then, that the League decided to co-operate with the Communists in ousting the Kuomintang. What is surprising, in the light of my interview and of developments since then, is that Mr. Lo, having co-operated with the Communists since 1949, has quite apparently failed to stick strictly to the role the League should play as defined by the Communists. "The central task the League sets itself," according to the Communists, "is to unite and remold the intellectuals, particularly the intellectuals of the middle and higher levels in cultural and educational fields, so that they may better serve China's Socialist construction."

During my conversation with Mr. Lo, I adjudged him a complete fellow-traveler, since his statements seemed to indicate that he had gone through considerable ideological remolding himself. There was nothing noteworthy to report as a result of our "political" interview; most of it was devoted to a discussion of Communism, but the words used by Mr. Lo were identical with those parroted by other government officials. China, he informed me, was going to be transformed by Communism. It was going to become a Socialist, industrial country. A brief discussion of the Hungarian situation was terminated by Mr. Lo's insistence that counter-revolutionaries had attempted to overthrow a regime which the Hungarian people supported. Since Mr. Lo spent several years in the United States—he obtained his Ph.D. at Columbia University —I asked him whether his experience with democracy in that country might not have suggested to him there was an alternative to Communism; that perhaps democracy, if given an opportunity, might have been good for China. "Only Communism can make China a strong country," was Mr. Lo's reply.

The ironical part of the conversation was that Mr. Lo insisted there was complete freedom of speech in China and cited the rectification program as evidence that the people of China are free to criticize their government. The extent of this so-called freedom of speech has since become apparent to Mr. Lo in a manner probably not contemplated by him on the day of our talk. He now stands accused of forming a sinister plot to overthrow the Communist party, for having expressed doubts as to the party being good for China. He has said that these doubts arose after reading anti-Soviet articles in British and American magazines and reports on happenings in Poland and Hungary.

In one respect, at least, the Communists have kept the official pledge they gave last May that no one should fear reprisal for voicing criticism. The pledge was given in these words: "The party has extended a cordial invitation to join in the rectification program if they like, with the assurance that they are free to withdraw again any time they like." In the spirit of this pledge, Mr. Lo has now made a confession (according to Peking reports) that he might have thought there was something wrong with the Communist leadership, but he continues to deny that he was involved in a political alliance to replace the party. The latest news reports are that Mr. Lo is being urged to do a little more confessing. He is being given the opportunity to withdraw from the rectification program.

The future of Mr. Lo is obviously in doubt, but it seems unlikely that the Communists will eliminate him and thus destroy any validity the rectification program may still have in the minds of the Chinese masses. It is more likely that Mr. Lo will make the confession required of him and in Communist China that is usually sufficient. The Communists strongly adhere to the principle that confession is good for the soul. Mr. Lo's future was probably best described by Premier Chou En-lai when he discussed the situation recently before the People's Congress. He was referring to people of Mr. Lo's ilk when he talked about some non-Communists who fail to devote enough effort to the duties that go with their posts. "These people," the Premier said, "stand aloof from and look askance at Communist party organizations and members. . . . We must make energetic efforts to correct them." He concluded by saying: "Some non-Communist members who are still inclined to oppose Socialism should particularly make greater efforts to remold themselves and rid themselves of such sentiments."

SATIRE IN THE CINEMA

CHANGCHUN (HSINKING). The hand of the Japanese lay heavily on northeast China during the fourteen years they occupied it. Nowhere is the evidence of their tenure more apparent than in this city. The architecture is predominantly Japanese. The hotel, the Kiring Guesthouse, was built by the Japanese, with the result that its bathtubs, beds, and the heelless slippers still thoughtfully provided by the Chinese management are Lilliputian by Western standards, especially for a Canadian standing more than six feet. Mirrors and sinks are set low to accommodate the Japanese.

My attention was directed by K. C. Wong, my interpreter, to scattered ruins in an isolated field on the outskirts of the city. This, he solemnly asserted, had been the site of a bacteria warfare factory operated by the Japanese and destroyed by them just before the Russians moved in to accept their surrender in August, 1945. Near by, a concrete pillar thrust high into the air. On closer examination it proved to be a crematorium where dead Japanese officers were consigned to their gods. A more utilitarian future is planned for the pillar by the Communists: they are going to convert it into a parachute tower and construct a public park around its base. The Japanese influence could not be escaped even when we stood on the sun deck of a recently finished geological institute. The building, Prof. Hu Lun Tze explained, stood on a foundation constructed by the Japanese. It was to have been a palace and, as such, occupied the most suitable and attractive site in the area.

On the way to the Northeast Film Studios, we drove along broad, paved streets with unusually large intersections, another heritage from the Japanese, and as we pulled into the entrance to a pile of gaunt cement buildings, it was to learn that these too had been constructed by the sons of Nippon. The assurances of Ho Fung Ling, chief secretary of the studios, that the studio, formerly the Tung Pi, had been reconstructed by the Chinese after they moved into it left me wondering about the conditions under which the Japanese had worked, if the present state of the buildings is an improvement on that era.

We gingerly picked our way along muddy laneways, up broken board steps, and into dirty, wet corridors to visit each of the six large filming studios, which themselves had dirt floors and roofs through which many cracks permitted a clear view of the sky.

Some movies were in production at the time of my visit. One film, *The Footsteps of Youth*, is the story of a designing department and scarcely strays away from the party line. It relates the struggles of a factory manager who must reject the design submitted by the girl he loves because it is too fancy and costly. The other film deals with *The Remarriage of Madam Lu*, a situation which could only have been possible following the introduction by the Communists of the Marriage Law in 1950. Prior to that, widows were discouraged from remarrying.

The studios have, however, produced two movies cast in lighter vein. Both these movies illustrate the trend away from the heavily propagandized productions which have come in for widespread criticism in the Chinese press. They have been permitted as part of Mao Tse-tung's current rectification campaign which is itself an indication that the Chinese are tiring of a steady diet of dogmatism.

One result of taking chairman Mao's suggestion at its face value is a delightful satire, *Before the New Chief Arrives*, and a fluffy bit of nonsense called *The Man Who Didn't Care About Trifles*. I had the pleasure of viewing both these films in movie houses here and in Peking, and the aid of an interpreter was not really necessary. The plots could be fully understood and enjoyed despite the difference in language. *Before the New Chief Arrives* is directed at the defects of China's present system. The story begins in a government bureau, in a hustle and bustle of preparations for the imminent arrival of its new chief. The hero (the administration officer) is described in a review as a smug bureaucrat who struts self-importantly among his subordinates but tries to curry favor with his superior (the new chief). Administration Officer Niu decides that a former storeroom should be redecorated as the incoming chief's office. He himself plans to move into the one vacated by the former chief which is, of course, better than the one Niu himself previously occupied. Niu also busies himself having streamers of welcome plastered all over the walls, all signed by him. The new chief, when he arrives, has the appearance of a caretaker and is mistaken for such by Niu. The film ends on the embarrassment of Niu, who tells the supposed caretaker how he and the new chief had fought together in guerilla wars and worked together in the land reform.

China Reconstructs, a magazine in English, reports that press and audiences alike applauded the long-overdue arrival of a satirical film. The magazine said that one critic thought the punch of the comedy was cushioned by too much slapstick for pure laughs. Another wrote that the static performance of the new chief, who appeared mildly amused at everything, took the bite out of some of the scenes. The director of the film confessed that he had pulled his punches in the production. "The satire had been more penetrating on the stage," he said, but he had been afraid of overstepping what some might think were the bounds between satire and slander. The magazine concludes its review with the comment that the audiences, however, know what is good and what is bad in life in China today. "It is true that they won't stand for libels on our new reality. But they want more and stronger satires directed at defects—with plenty of pepper in them."

The Man Who Didn't Care About Trifles relates the confusion caused by an absent-minded poet who unconsciously makes trouble for everybody but himself by violating the rules of common courtesy while lost in a cloud of poetic creation. He throws debris on the streets; carves his initials on an ancient pillar in a park; picks the flowers in a park, and ignores no smoking signs and admonitions to be quiet in a public library. The unhappy result of it all for the poet is the loss of the girl who has secretly admired him, and the film fades out with the young man shrugging his shoulders and saying, "All is lost."

These films and many others produced here and at Shanghai do not go far toward satisfying the demands of a domestic audience numbered in the hundreds of millions, all of whom look upon their visits to the cinema as their main source of entertainment. It is also about all they can afford, and admission is comparatively cheap—25 and 30 fen (10 and 12 cents Canadian). The result is that the bulk of the films the Chinese now see are foreign, and dubbing in new sound tracks is a major occupation of the film studios. Since 1949 the studios here have produced 67 feature films and handled 301 films which have been given Chinese sound tracks. An additional phase of the work is the conversion of Chinese films into sound tracks for the national minorities, of which there are 47, belonging to four distinct linguistic families.

COUNTRYSIDE AND COAL MINE

FUSHUN. It was a lovely bright June Sunday when we (Mrs. Chang Chin Shen, my interpreter, and Ying Yu Fang, the driver, and I), set out to have a look at the famed open-pit coal mines of this district. We were in a Packard 120, a late-forties model. Behind us we had left Shenyang (Mukden) with its colorful blend of Chinese, Japanese, and Russian architecture. The last is perhaps best illustrated by a cold, concrete column, built by the Russians in 1945 to commemorate their all-too-easy liberation of the city from the Japanese. It was the one edifice clearly visible from my room in a hotel which was of Japanese origin. The Chinese contribution to the cosmopolitan atmosphere consisted of two basketball stands in the middle of a lawn which graced the front of the hotel property.

Northeast China is populated by a people closely akin in appearance to our own Indians and Eskimos. Once away from the city atmosphere, bowling along an excellent paved highway, and regaled by whiffs of new-mown hay, it is not at all difficult to view the gently rolling farmland as being typical of the Canadian countryside in Quebec and Ontario in the month of June. Occasionally I was brought sharply back to reality as we sped by groups of Chinese at the roadside. With faded blue jeans rolled to the knees, vari-colored cotton singlets open and flapping in the breeze, and with heads, crowned with straw hats, bent low, they toiled in the time-honored Chinese fashion to move their produce on two-wheeled vehicles for which they supplied the sole motive power. Realization, too, of just exactly where I was, came as we frequently drove through tiny villages, all presenting the same flat brown vista of straw huts plastered with mud to repel the elements. And each tiny hovel—for that is all they were—had the inevitable wall, sometimes constructed of mud or made simply of corn stalks stuck in the earth, for it is characteristic of a Chinese, regardless of his station in life, not to present his front door to the passing world.

Here and there red splashes disturbed the green horizon. These were the three-story red-brick dormitories that new China builds for the workers and sometimes for the peasants. All the dormitories look like peas in a pod, since undoubtedly necessity has prompted the use of a single plan for the thousands of such buildings which dot China's landscape. Generally grouped in clusters of a dozen or so, they attract to themselves nothing but hard-packed earth. Not even a blade of grass is able to survive the incessant pounding of the feet of the thousands who occupy them, since families of four or five are normal in one room no bigger than the bedroom of an average-sized Canadian apartment. These Chinese flats can accommodate up to 200 families.

Fushun is said to be the smokiest town in China, but it was such a bright cloudless day that not even the smoke pouring out of its coking furnaces did much to discourage the sun from shining on it. As we approached the city, the pleasant green of the countryside almost imperceptibly and grudgingly yielded to the industrial blight which blackens all coal mining centers. A long, narrow bridge, barely wide enough for two vehicles to pass, was bulging with pedestrians, pedicabs, laborers toting loads on their backs, and others pulling and pushing at wagons heaped high with goods. Mostly by a combination of constant horn-blowing and sheer luck, our driver bulled his way through the crowd, edged by a bus on the wrong side of the road, and roared into the main street. Here everything except the people was black. The wooden shacks that lined both sides of a black, graveled road and serve both as business and living quarters were black. Even some of the clothing worn by the hundreds that squatted and lolled about the street corners seemed dull and lifeless, as if in tune with the general surroundings. Far ahead we could see the coal-lift of the Fushun mines rearing into the sky, but to get to it we had to weave our way over dusty roads, scattering pedestrians and livestock alike by the blaring of the car's horn; our driver seemed determined that nothing should delay our progress even for a second.

The open-pit coal mine here is reported to be one of the largest in the world and it has been in active production since 1914. Because it was Sunday, not all of the mine's 16,000 workers were on the job. Only 2,000 were working, clearing away shale and sand, and they were so lost in the vast hole dug in the ground that their presence and activity were scarcely visible. We viewed the gash left by forty-three years of mining

from the sky deck of the administration building perched precariously at the side of the big hole. We could see across the
vast terraced slash in the rolling land to where what looked
like toy trains chugged around the perimeter at various levels,
carting away the sand and shale so sufficient coal would be
exposed for the next week's operations. The hole in the ground
is more than four miles long, almost a mile across at its widest
point, and half a mile where it is narrowest. The coal, which is
covered by layers of shale, green shale, and sand, averages
about thirty feet in depth. A subsidiary product of the mine,
which produces a hard, long-burning anthracite, is oil obtained from the shale which has about the same depth as the
coal vein. The shale is shipped to a nearby refinery for processing.

Despite a high degree of mechanization introduced during
the past eight years, the mine, contrary to Chinese government
claims, is not producing as much coal as it did under Japanese
occupation. Perhaps the mine secretary let a statistical cat out
of the bag when he admitted that last year's production of
3,840,000 tons was not as high as during the occupation
years. Government sources publicly claim that there has been
a fantastic (this is the government's language) increase in
production at Fushun. The explanation appears to be a simple
and a reasonable one. The mine is now so deep that more time
is consumed in getting the coal to the top.

TRAIN TRIP

ANSHAN. It is the proud boast of China's Communist regime
that the new order has turned this country's teeming millions
into a polite nation. In the cities there is considerable evidence

to support the claim that persistent prodding has developed in the Chinese an "After You, My Dear Alphonse" attitude toward their fellow Chinese. They form into orderly lines, often a block long, for buses; they are attentive to the elderly, assisting them on and off street cars and buses and opening doors for them. All of this, according to those experienced in things Chinese, is a refreshing and a decided change from the behavior of former days.

That this newly acquired politeness is only a thin veneer is nowhere more evident than at railway stations. There is no denying that China has made considerable progress toward extending her railway lines and putting new equipment on the road. These efforts, it would seem, have barely kept up with the increase in population, so that space on trains is at a premium.

Two types of accommodation are available on Chinese trains: hard and soft; and they fit their description. The hard seat is just plain varnished board, with a back of the same material; the soft seat is equivalent in quality, comfort, and appearance to the Canadian equipment which was dragged out of mothballs and pressed into service during the war years. Chinese coaches provide half hard-seat accommodation and half soft. The same division and the same choice of comfort is found in the sleeper cars, except that there are four soft berths to a soft compartment and six sleeping places to a hard compartment. I can testify, after a brief personal encounter with the latter, that their cheapness is no recommendation.

The Chinese are an adaptable race; they take conditions as they exist and that is why every railway station, except perhaps those in Peking, seems to attract hundreds of Chinese of all ages, who sprawl about on the pavement, curl up in shaded corners, and sometimes reach a density which makes it difficult to distinguish between pavement and bodies. It doesn't necessarily follow that all of these people are waiting to catch a train. Some have nothing more to do. One advantage of choosing a railway station at which to do nothing is that there is always some activity to brighten waking moments, even if it is nothing more than the strident shouts of the food peddlers who seem to materialize out of thin air just as a train pulls into the station.

Mrs. Chang Chin Shen (my interpreter) and myself had made a two-hour, comfortable morning run to this city from Shenyang, sitting on soft seats in a half-filled coach that gave no hint of what the return trip was to be like. It apparently had not occurred to Mrs. Chang to inform me, until just before we reached the station early that evening, that only hard seats were available on the way back. The first hint that a completely new traveling experience was about to be my lot came when we arrived at the station. It was so densely packed with humanity that it looked for all the world like a midway on Labor Day. My initial reaction was that surely not all of these people were waiting for the same train. This reaction was quickly corrected by Mrs. Chang, who informed me these were workers from the iron and steel works of this area and they were on their way home.

My experience in traveling in China has taught that the most desirable quality a foreigner can acquire is that of patience. Be patient, do not fret, and China Intourist and the astonishing solicitude of Chinese officialdom that foreigners should not be inconvenienced will take care of any problem, whatever its apparent magnitude. So it was in this complacent frame of mind that I elbowed my way onto the platform, hard on the heels of Mrs. Chang, who is only about the size of a minute but did a most effective job breaking trail. Our progress toward the rails was only impeded by the fact that most Chinese are so curious when a foreigner appears in their midst that they tend to swarm around him to get a closer look. The only danger inherent in this oft-repeated and close scrutiny is that the Chinese are inveterate handshakers. They'll grasp another's hand and wring it at the slightest excuse, and it is always a temptation to confirm what seems to be a friendly situation by shaking the nearest hand. This is a fatal gesture in a crowd of more than a dozen or so, since the hands of all present must be shaken until everyone has had a chance at cementing the friendship.

While I was mentally resisting the urge to break the monotony of being peered at by hundreds of eyes, by tempting fate with a handshake, Mrs. Chang was deep in consultation with two platform constables. As the train rolled in, she grabbed me by the arm and down the platform we went, on the double, with the two constables ahead, parting the mass of humanity that opened just enough to permit us to pass and then closed in behind us. The train stopped, other police held back the mob until the conductors had alighted, and then, swish, it happened. Every door was instantly jammed tight with bodies. Elbows flew out, shoulders pushed, and the law of the jungle operated. Age, health, sex, none of these meant anything. Those who pushed the hardest got in first. Although it was obvious that there were more people than seats, my faith in Intourist did not waver except to the degree that I considered it quite possible we would have to wait for a later train.

My faith was justified. With Mrs. Chang leading the way, I pushed my way up the steps of a coach and turned sharp right, to find it packed to the doors except for two empty seats from which a constable restrained the mob with outstretched arms. Not a little embarrassed, I took the inside seat at the urging of Mrs. Chang, who sat down beside me. The opposite seat was immediately occupied by two women, carrying infant children. They had no sooner settled themselves than they both opened the fronts of their dresses and proceeded to nurse the children. A few steps away another woman was busy performing the same necessary duty, and I made a gesture toward getting up and letting her have my seat. I was restrained from doing so by Mrs. Chang, who later explained that had I given my seat to the nursing mother I would have earned the enmity of all the other men in the coach. They would have resented my getting up, since they would have felt obliged to follow my example. Chinese women, Mrs. Chang added, are now the equal of men, by law, and they take their chances, the same as anyone else. It was not difficult to refrain from shattering this new Chinese tradition.

Like any commuter train in any other part of the world, our train stopped at every little station along the way and the Chinese poured out, many carrying lunch boxes. As the train pulled away I could see them picking their way along mud roads to tiny villages, most of which lay some distance from the railway tracks. We arrived at Shenyang at 8:59 P.M. after a 6:26 P.M. departure. During the intervening time the train made stops at thirteen stations.

POLIO VACCINE

PEKING. China is well launched on a twelve-year program to eliminate polio. The chief weapon being used is similar to the Salk anti-polio vaccine which the Chinese claim is not known to them. The chief difference between the two methods is that the Chinese use mice brains as the base of the vaccine culture which they developed here in research which began in 1950, whereas in the Salk method the kidney cells of rhesus monkeys from India are used to grow the virus.

It seemed incredible that the Chinese Ministry of Health, which has available to it medical journals from all countries, including Canada and the United States, had not heard of the Salk discovery, as I indicated to Dr. S. F. Chiang, spokesman for the group of five doctors who turned up for the interview I had requested. Dr. Chiang consulted with his colleagues at length and, turning to me, shook his head. "This Salk method is not known to us," he declared.

My efforts to determine whether the Chinese have actually developed an anti-polio vaccine which would appear to be much simpler and cheaper than the Salk method had begun several weeks earlier, when I first appeared at the Ministry of Health seeking a story on the over-all health program of China. At that time the discussion gravitated to polio and its pre- ventives, and the Chinese informed me that they were using a vaccine which was developed by injecting the virus into embryo chickens. Since the advantages of such a method were obvious by comparison with the use of kidneys from monkeys, which had to be imported, I was all ears. However, I found it difficult to elicit any further details from Dr. Chiang, who con- tinued to insist that he was unaware of the Salk discovery.

I arranged to pursue the point at a later date if I could obtain more information on the Salk method. Thanks to the reasonable speed of Chinese air mail, and to the quick response of James S. Band, Deputy Minister of Welfare for the province of Ontario, to whom I directed my request, I was able to present the Chinese with detailed information on the Salk method, the time of its discovery, and also the skepticism expressed by Ontario doctors as to the validity of the Chinese claim that anti-polio vaccine can be propagated in an embryo chicken.

Dr. Chiang read this material and it was then that he changed the story and first mentioned the use of mice brains, still insisting, however, that he had never heard of Salk. The Chinese, Dr. Chiang added, are still experimenting with the use of chicken embryo as a base in which to cultivate the polio virus. He admitted that so far this method has not been successful. The development of the vaccine produced from mice brains continued through 1950 to 1952, Dr. Chiang said, and the first controlled inoculations were given in that year.

Briefly, the Chinese process consists of injecting the polio virus into the brains of month-old white mice. The brains are put through a chopping process as are the monkey kidneys in the Salk method, and after a period of time the culture is sterilized with formaldehyde. Three injections of the vaccine are given at intervals of three weeks and apparently the amount varies according to the age of the recipient. Children get a larger dose than older people. A booster shot is required annually. This program is free of charge, Dr. Chiang said, and is at present confined largely to cities and towns, since facilities for refrigeration are seldom available in the countryside.

The program has grown from 8,000 in 1952 to 4 million this year. In 1955 and 1956, about 3 million inoculations were given and about 1½ million in each of 1953 and 1954. Of 200,000 children inoculated in Peking, only four showed a reaction and these were mild cases of polio, Dr. Chiang said.

In addition to using the current vaccine and continuing experiments with the use of embryo chickens, the Chinese are investigating the possibility that some of the herbs used by Chinese herbal doctors, who far outnumber the medical men, may be effective in preventing polio. Details are lacking as to just what herb is being used in the experiments, but Dr. Chiang said that if it lives up to advance claims it can be taken orally. At least, that's his story. In addition to their work with vaccines, the Chinese are concentrating on research to prove their contention that the mosquito is the carrier of the polio germ.

FLYING BY SIGN LANGUAGE

SHENYANG. "Ching ne yao kuo chi lui Hsing sheh. Weh shi chia na ta chi cheh. Weh yao chao lui kuen." This is phonetic Chinese, and simply illustrates one of the safety devices resorted to by a foreigner traveling alone in China. Literally translated, it identifies me as a Canadian correspondent. It requests that the local China Intourist office be advised of my presence and that I want to go to a hotel. Despite the almost too efficient attention given foreigners in China by Intourist, there inevitably comes the moment when a visitor finds himself on his own, simply because it is not practical or economical to have an interpreter along to lead him by the hand.

So it was that I found myself completely on my own and on my way to northeast China, the area in which the Japanese established a puppet monarchy in 1931. Pu Yi, the boy emperor they placed on the throne, is still in the area. He's in a jail near Fushun but my efforts to see him when I was in that area were rewarded only with a polite grin and a shrug of the shoulders. The Japanese changed the name of the area from Manchuria to Manchoukuo, a sore point with the Chinese —so much so that they now refer to it only as northeast China.

Having been safely put aboard the aircraft by Mr. Yen, my Peking interpreter and constant companion, without whose aid I must admit it would have been impossible to thread my way through the devious Chinese government channels, I settled down in one of the six seats (the rest of the space is used for cargo) to look forward to having a decent meal at Shenyang. A 7:00 A.M. departure had permitted a breakfast consisting only of a hot Chinese tea, without milk or sugar. That's all that was available at the airport and the hotel dining room was not operating when we left at 6:15 A.M.

96

My air companions included two foreigners, identified as Russians by their bell-bottomed trousers, who were astonishingly rude to all they dealt with, Chinese and foreigners alike. Of all the foreigners who frequent China these days, the Russians and the East Germans seem to attempt to outdo each other in being taciturn to such a degree that it makes life most unpleasant for those who must necessarily rub shoulders with them. To make matters worse, one of the Russians assaulted my nostrils and my empty stomach by hauling a huge chunk of foul-smelling and evil-looking cheese and a hunk of dry black bread from his briefcase. With the aid of the big blade of a jackknife he shoveled strips of cheese and pieces of bread into him. A brief spell of rough weather added to all this made a resort to the air-sickness bag a distinct possibility. Luckily, my lengthy record of having a cast-iron stomach in the air remained inviolate as we bumped down onto the runway in pouring rain at Shenyang airport, located several miles outside the city and strongly garrisoned by Chinese troops.

Shenyang is a difficult word to pronounce and a strange one to foreigners, since this city is commonly known to them as Mukden. How that name came to be is a mystery incapable of being solved here, since the many Chinese questioned about it simply reply: "We have always called it Shenyang. Only foreigners refer to it as Mukden." It was about 11:00 A.M. when we climbed through the rear door of a small Russian-built bus, joined by several Chinese who had apparently been waiting for just such a ride, and were transported about a mile, bumping our way over mud roads to a string of what appeared to be army huts. Here we dashed into the rain and out of it again into a dilapidated lunchroom, featured mainly by broken floor boards which exposed a hole, about four feet square, which had to be skirted carefully, and small chairs without backs, grouped around a few tables.

A huge bowl of what appeared to be spinach soup with two

whole hard-boiled eggs floating in it, was placed before me, together with four thick slices of bread, but no butter. I had barely worked my way through the soup, which was delicious, but filling, when there was placed before me a plate heaped high with slabs of meat and fried potatoes. The soup had satisfied my appetite, and I sat at the table rudely, I must confess, gaping at the Chinese shoveling rice into them with their chopsticks, when the waiter, all decked out in a white cap that dropped down below his ears, and a white apron that all but hid his shoes, beckoned me to accompany him outside. Into the rain we went again and threaded our way around mud holes to a door identified by the number three. I was ushered into a wallpapered room containing four cots, no chairs, and one lone electric light bulb hanging from the ceiling. As I turned to the waiter in some astonishment, he placed the palms of his hands together, put them to his cheek, and inclined his head, obviously suggesting that I should get some sleep. That was at 12:30 in the afternoon, and so far not a word had been exchanged other than a brief fruitless attempt at the outset to determine if any of the many Chinese in the vicinity understood English. The sleeping gesture, together with the continuing rain and thunder, added up to a delayed flight. And it was delayed until the following morning, as I subsequently determined through repeated pointing to the sky and the numerals on my watch. Unable to return to the aircraft, where I had unsuspectingly left all my belongings, I idled the afternoon hours away by leafing through Chinese magazines. At 6:00 P.M. the waiter in white reappeared with a call to dinner. No order was taken and none offered, and a plate with six huge slabs of meat was set before me, followed, strangely enough, rather than preceded, by another huge bowl of soup in which floated unidentifiable materials. One hunk of meat and half a bowl of soup later I returned to the barrack room, with the distinct impression we were to be awakened at

5:00 A.M. for an early takeoff. And so we were awakened—by the blaring of a loudspeaker—promptly at 5:00 A.M., and a look through the doorway disclosed hundreds of China's new young soldiers doing setups in the dawn's early light. A breakfast of six eggs floating face up in grease on one plate, two hunks of dry bread, and Chinese tea ended my association with the cuisine of Shenyang airport.

On the return from Harbin I traveled by train to Changchun and Shenyang, and it was the hectic moments following my arrival at the railway station in Shenyang that emphasized the necessity of adding to my Chinese vocabulary. None of the Chinese stations is identified in anything except the national language, so a traveler can only assume that, if the train is on schedule, he is at the right place if he gets there at the normal hour of arrival. It was 12:30 in the morning when I stepped down to the station platform and looked in vain for an Intourist face. I had waited around for about three minutes when I was collared by a policeman who firmly steered me into the station reception room and there indicated he would like to see my documents. I showed him all of them, including my passport; he thumbed through it and seemed more interested in the proof attached to it of the necessary inoculations than in anything he could read. The battle to acquaint him with my situation lasted about a quarter of an hour, and it was aided and abetted by close to fifteen spectators who came from somewhere out of the night, displaying the usual curiosity of the Chinese when their ears catch an indication of an argument. It was just at the moment when your weary correspondent had become reconciled to spending the night either in the station or in jail that a woman's voice announced the arrival of an Intourist representative. She was Mrs. Chang Chin Shen, full of apologies.

The next morning, with her guidance, the first order of business was to devise some method of avoiding experiences similar to those which had occurred at Shenyang's airport and railway station. My opening sentences are part of a carefully prepared glossary about to be put to the acid test during four weeks of almost continual traveling—on my own.

TAMING THE YELLOW RIVER

AT THE SANMEN DAM. China sees the problem of the Yellow River as the concern of the whole nation. The Yellow is the second greatest river in China; it is more than 3,000 miles long and its basin has an area of almost 290,000 square miles. It was the cradle of Chinese civilization and for a long time the political and economic center of the nation. According to 1954 statistics, 40 per cent of China's cultivated area is in the Yellow basin, and the wheat growing area of that 40 per cent forms 61.7 per cent of all the country's wheat fields. The percentage for miscellaneous cereals ranges from 37 to 63; cotton, 57; and tobacco, 67. The Yellow River has vast sources of cheap electric power which could be developed at a tenth of what it costs to produce thermo-electric power in China today. Its possibilities as a source of water for irrigation have barely been tapped either, nor can it be navigated by modern river shipping, so important in China. Only wooden boats capable of carrying from ten to seventy-five tons, and inflated skin rafts, are in use on separate and isolated sections.

What is more, the Yellow River often becomes a menace not only to its own basin but to all of China. Most of the floods that it causes are the result of heavy rains in the summer, but some start from heavy rains in September and October, and some from melted snow in March and April. But the extraordinary seriousness of the Yellow floods is due even more to the silt deposited in the lower reaches. The Yellow River is thick with loess, the yellow fertile soil which gives the river its name, and there is an old Chinese saying: "If you get into the Yellow River, you never get clean again." The river has a greater concentration of silt than any other stream in the world—thirty-four times more than the Nile and ten times more than the Colorado in the United States. The amount it carries to the sea on an average every year is 1,380,000 tons, or enough sediment to build a wall a yard high and a yard wide around the world twenty-three times. In the lower reaches, where the drop is gentler, this silt cannot all flow into the sea, but settles in large quantities. As a result, the river bed has gradually risen until its mean level between dikes is now higher than the surrounding country. It is, in fact, an elevated river in many places. Because of the continuing deposit of silt, the river frequently changes course in its lower reaches and that is where the most serious floods occur. According to records which go back more than 3,000 years, there have been inundations and breaches in the dikes on more than 1,500 occasions on the lower reaches, and there were twenty-six changes in course, nine of them major. In 1933, floods caused more than fifty breaches in the dikes, and jeopardized more than 3,640,000 people, 18,000 of whom were killed. Property worth about 230 million yuan (about $90 million Canadian at today's rate of exchange) was destroyed. The government also claims that in 1938 the Kuomintang government, in an offensive against the Communists, opened dikes near Chengchow and caused the death of 890 thousand persons. The government is attempting to hold the flood line with temporary dikes until the major project of taming the river is more advanced, but it is admitted that the Yellow's rapid silting cannot be dealt with by piling up and reinforcing dikes. Diking becomes a vicious circle. The higher and stronger the dikes, the quicker the silt is deposited, because it has no way of escaping. Since the floods and silt of the lower reaches come primarily from the middle reaches, which so badly need this water and soil, the problem is to control the water and soil in the middle area.

The government has a two-phase plan. It proposes to build a series of dams and reservoirs on the main river and its tributaries so that soil and water can be conserved, flooding prevented, the volume of water regulated, and irrigation, navigation, and power developed. The second phase is the conservation of soil and water on a large scale, chiefly in Kansu, Shensi, and Shansi provinces, where the loss of water and soil is most serious. Everywhere, section by section, from highland to gully, from tributary to main river, water is to be stored and soil retained. Everything possible is to be done to use the river water for industry, agriculture, and transport, and to leave loess and rain water where they are needed—on the farmland. The main feature of the comprehensive plan is what the government calls the Staircase Plan to build a series of dams on the main river so that the levels will form a sort of staircase. This work will be done in four sections; and forty-six dams are to be constructed. Sanmen dam is the first step in this staircase. Parallel to this, many reservoirs will be built in the main Yellow tributaries. A few of these will be multiple-purpose works, but most of them are intended primarily to retain silt. Until conservation schemes are successful in reducing the flow of soil into the Yellow, many of the dams will tend to silt up, but the main structure, the Sanmen, is designed to hold all the silt that would normally be carried down the river over a period of fifty to seventy years. That is the reason for its height—about 350 feet.

My first glimpse of the Yellow River came as we eased by a bulldozer on a hairpin turn. We had made our way about twenty miles down the valley from the railway station at Huei

Hsing, which is the staging area for the mountains of equipment needed to construct the Sanmen dam. We were on the tortuous new road, carved out of huge hills of loess, over which the equipment will be transported to the dam. Sometimes we dropped into mud holes in which it seemed for the moment that the car would be lost, and we had to navigate a long tunnel down which streams of water were flowing—the aftermath of a brief morning shower.

It is difficult to describe the appearance of the Yellow River valley, for erosion has worked queer tricks. It has fashioned walls that would be taken for man's handiwork if they did not stand alone in a desolation of gullies. The gullies are so deep (600 to 700 feet) that they defy access even to the enterprising Chinese, whose agricultural ingenuity is nowhere so effectively demonstrated as in the intense cultivation of the pin-sized plateaus that have been left standing by centuries of erosion. As the gullies kept increasing in number and widening, the flat land gradually disappeared and turned into countless long ridges and domes. In a few places where the erosion is worst, most of the soil even on some of the hillocks has been lost, and they have become barren stone hills. This process has been going on uninterrupted for generations, gradually reducing the arable land in the area, cutting down the fertility of the soil and the yield of crops. The excessive number of gullies, their steep slopes, the lack of forest and pasture to retain water, and the lack of ponds and lakes to store it were all a vivid illustration of the loss of rainfall to the river. The land was parched in appearance less than an hour after a heavy downpour, but the gullies still retained lingering streamlets.

The car took us to within a mile of the site where 2,000 workers were working around the clock to prepare the river bed for the construction of a coffer dam. They were trying to demolish a huge deposit of rock, and if they did not succeed within a few weeks (and it seemed unlikely that they would), all operations would have to be moved to higher ground for four months while the river was in flood. We weaved our way over two bamboo suspension bridges, swinging precariously above the river. They were strung from rock outcroppings which still retain their Chinese names—Gate of God and Gate of Man—given by those Chinese who, for thousands of years, have used the Yellow River as a route of commerce. On the way, we passed laborers with bags of cement tied on their backs and other workmen pushing and tugging to haul huge pieces of heavy machinery and loads of piping to the job. Everything is brought to the staging site by rail and then trucked to the river, but manpower is used to get it across to the working area.

High up on the cliffs, drillers were kicking up a dust preparatory to blowing the top off a rock mound; below, a steam shovel was working side by side with laborers, toting two wicker baskets on a yoke, to load the debris of a previous blast into trucks. Here and there gangs of straw-hatted workers were toiling away with shovels and their wicker baskets, eating into the cliff of loess to find a firm foundation of rock to which the dam could be attached. So deep is the gorge at this point that when I looked to the west, the toiling Chinese resembled ants patiently filing up and down paths worn smooth by the feet of men who had made thousands of such trips. The analogy seemed even more appropriate as I watched other Chinese popping in and out of holes in the wall of the cliff, for a good part of the population in this area lives in caves carved out of the solid loess. Some, but not all, of these cave homes have brick fronts. For the most part their occupants have relied on the traditional tenacity of loess which hardens to a solid mass when worked with water. All along the highway to the dam site were frequent illustrations of the peculiar qualities of loess. When it is cultivated, it can produce up to three crops a year in this area, but when it is packed smooth, the result is as permanent as any plaster or cement job. Yet, strangely enough, lacking the touch of the hand of man, loess deposits have a natural looseness that makes them particularly susceptible to erosion.

In 1963, when the Sanmen dam is completed, it will create an artificial lake with an area of 1,400 square miles, and dislodge from their homes 870 thousand persons. At the current rate of population increase in China, this figure will be close to a million in 1963. When I suggested to Wung Ching Fu, chief of the technical department on the dam project, that this presented a difficult problem in human relations, he shrugged his shoulders and replied: "What does it matter when it is for the good of the 80 million to 100 million people who live in the Yellow River plain?" In this, Mr. Wung was simply reflecting the official view that, regardless of the immediate discomfort of what after all is a comparatively small portion of China's huge population, nothing must stand in the way of the successful completion of the most important project now being undertaken by China. So far as moving the people is concerned, the government, Mr. Wung explained, will provide for that. Materials for constructing new houses will be supplied and the prospective occupants will do the work.

The Sanmen dam is the first phase of the huge project and it has four purposes. Flood control is the most important and will be the first completed. Then will follow a power plant, capable of producing 1,100,000 kilowatts, to supply the energy which will be required by the new industrial area that is being developed to the north and west of the gorge. The third phase of the dam will be a spillway, and, lastly, a retaining wall. Initially the population of the new industrial area will be the people destined to be uprooted by the artificial lake. They will be farmers, and will be shifted gradually. As a matter of fact, some of the younger men are already in the new area constructing an irrigation system—a prime necessity in Chinese agricultural activities.

Most of the men involved in the planning of the project and many of those now actively working on it will not see its completion, even if it takes no more than the estimated fifty years needed finally to control the river. It is their hope, however, that when their plan is completed, the Yellow River will no longer be known as China's sorrow; that the age-old dream will come true—the Yellow River will run clear.

SIAN REBORN

CHANGAN (SIAN). This ancient capital of early civilized China is being reborn in response to the needs of a vast new industrial area the Chinese are planning to the north and west of here. The new industrial area is now in its infancy, not much removed from the drawing board, but it will be built and maintained by close to one million people, whose present homes will be submerged by the great artificial lake that will be formed by the Sanmen dam. Sian will thrive on the vast movement and production of materials required to maintain the new population.

In its rebirth, Sian, more pointedly even than Canton, illustrates the contrast between the new and the old. Proud new buildings, most of them erected to house government and Communist party departments, and an ornate six-story hotel that sprawls over three average city blocks, are cast among the thousands of mud-walled huts where the Chinese live as they have lived for thousands of years. A great new road cuts a wide swath through the thickly clustered mud huts, all bearing witness to the value of the loess of the Yellow River for that unusual quality which gives it a cement-like appearance and the hardness of plaster. Often the squalid clusters of huts are lost to sight in the dust kicked up by vehicles on the new road. It is only a second-grade gravel road, but still the best in the area, and it will eventually be hard-surfaced.

Sian's historical background is enriched by its role as the capital city during eleven Chinese dynasties. Geographically its importance in China goes back to the western Chou dynasty, whose capital was at Kaoching (not far from here) in 1200 B.C. Sian lost its affinity to the state capital when the latter was moved to Loyi, not far from present-day Loyang, in 770 B.C. Sian (then known as Changan) re-entered the limelight in A.D. 618, when Li Yuan, leader of a peasant movement, founded the Tang dynasty and made this city his capital. From the reign of Tai Tsung (A.D. 627–649) to that of Hsuan Tsung (A.D. 712–756) the majority of the peasants received land under an equalization system introduced by Li Yuan and currently viewed by the Communists as the forerunner of their land reform system of taking from the landlords and giving to the tenants. Irrigation works were greatly developed and the economy of the countryside prospered. The state established many handicraft centers and the institution of a courier service and a system of post-horses facilitated trade. Sian, Loyang, Yangchow, and Canton became important trading centers. The Tang empire extended its influence into the northwest, bringing the broad stretches of territory in the north and south of the Tien Shan Mountains under control. Merchants and religious teachers from Arabia and other countries came to China. Sian had between 4,000 and 5,000 foreign residents and became the center of trade and culture.

Many brilliant Chinese poets claimed Sian as their home and among these Li Po, Tu Fu, and Po Chu-yi, all names familiar to present-day Chinese, were regarded as the greatest.

Still in use is a cobblestone bridge on the city's outskirts (we crossed it on our way to the nearby hot springs) which is still remembered as the place where Sian's poets said good-by to their visitors. The ritual, it is related here, was for the guests to be accompanied the few miles distance to the bridge and there, with great ceremony, to be bade farewell by their hosts. Sian was also the home of famous Chinese painters. Among these were Wu Tao-tse, figure painter, and Wang Wei, landscape artist.

Many forms of religious belief flourished freely in Sian, among them Zoroastrianism, which was introduced during the northern dynasties. Here also flourished the Nestorian Church, the first Christian church in China, which prospered during the seventh and eighth centuries of the Christian era. It is reported that princes had been enrolled in the church and that great ministers had contributed to its funds and restored its shrines. By the eighteenth century the religion had vanished, leaving no literary evidence of its existence other than a record on a stone slab. The slab was discovered by Christian missionaries from Europe when they first penetrated into western China. No explanation was available on the reasons for the waning and vanishing away of the religion.

At one time Sian had a population of more than 3 million, which dwindled during the passing centuries to a few thousands. Now the population is approaching 2 million, and the spreading out of the city led to the discovery of a further link with China's past. Chinese archeological organizations consider it the most exciting find in recent years. It is a complete Neolithic village at Pan Po, just east of here. It was uncovered during the building of Sian's three new textile mills (a fourth is under construction), and is the best preserved and one of the largest of several Neolithic sites excavated since 1949.

The settlement belonged to the Yangshao painted-pottery culture, supposed to have flourished around the second half of the third millennium B.C. From the discovery of the remains of millet in a covered pot and pottery kilns it has been concluded that the people lived a settled communal life. Besides farming (their main occupation), they hunted, fished, and gathered wild food. Their chief working tools were stone objects made by the polishing or flaking technique. They wove cloth, and used pottery for cooking and storage. Skills and arts were at a fairly high level. These early ancestors of today's Sian residents also raised domestic animals. Bones of swine, dogs, and sheep were found around the village. The people hunted with stone- or bone-tipped arrows, and with stone or pottery balls shot from slings. They fished with hook and line, and also with harpoons. As Sian's industrialization continues to encroach on the history-steeped, yellow acres of its suburbs, China's archeologists are hopeful of finding more evidence to link the city with the stone age.

HISTORIC BATHTUB

HUA CHING CHE. As I relaxed in a hot spring bath which had been the favorite resting place of Queen Yang Kuei Pei more than a thousand years ago, I couldn't help but think of another Chinese who has left his mark on the history of his country—Chiang Kai-shek. He too reclined in the same historic tub, located near the base of Li Shen Mountain. The Generalissimo, now confined to the bounds of Formosa, spent a great deal of time in this area, enjoying the comfort of its hot spring baths and the bracing mountain air as a relief from the sun-baked treeless plains.

There are certain landmarks at Li Shen which are virtual

shrines to the Chinese Communists. Before climbing to a pavilion which the Communists have erected on the side of the mountain, I relaxed over a cup of tea in the cottage in which Chiang Kai-shek had been sleeping one December night in 1936 when a bullet smashed through a front window. Chiang Kai-shek, without waiting to determine who was behind the bullet or if it was an accident, took off through a rear window and scuttled up the side of the mountain; he was found crouching in a hole, the site of which is now marked by the pavilion. Hundreds come daily to the cottage to see the hole (about the size of a quarter) in the window, and to see the bed, which still has the original mattress and bedclothes.

The story behind Chiang's night run is that in December, 1936, he was planning an extermination drive based not far from here in Sian, the capital of Shensi province, which had been all but overrun by the Communists. The army facing the Communists was composed of Manchurians led by Chang Hseuh-liang, son of the warlord Chang Tso-lin. The troops were all exiles from their home province and not any too anxious to fight the Communists who, they said, were more anxious to fight the Japanese. Rumors that there was disaffection amounting to a virtual armistice prompted Chiang to decide that personal intervention was necessary. Chiang and his staff went to Sian by air December 7, 1936, and arrived here December 12. That night the shot was fired, and Chiang learned a little later that it had been fired by the troops of Chang Hseuh-liang who had mutinied, and who had scrambled up the side of the mountain and surrounded Chiang's hiding spot. He returned, a prisoner, to the room he had just flown from, and remained a prisoner while he listened to the arguments of his erstwhile colleagues that he should make peace with the Communists and declare resistance to Japan. The arguments were long and heated, complicated by Chiang's refusal to pardon the rebels and the certain fact that if he persisted in this attitude he would never have an opportunity to pardon or punish. Ironically, one of the General's visitors, and a most persistent arguer, was Chou En-lai, now premier of Communist China, who had narrowly escaped with his life when Chiang ordered a crackdown of Communist strikers in 1927. Chou had been one of the chief organizers of the strike. Chou had several talks with the Kuomintang leader and finally convinced him that he had to accept the terms offered by the rebels and the Communists or he would be put to death. Chou also convinced Chiang that if he accepted the terms, the Communists would recognize him as head of the state. Chiang accepted the terms of amnesty for the rebels, an armistic and peace pact with the Communists, and a united front to oppose any further Japanese aggression.

It is just possible that Chiang now wonders if perhaps death in this Shensi hot spring resort might not have been preferable to going the way of those who get involved in a united front with the Communists. The details of the years that follow have no place here, but it is a fact that the united front ended in 1949 with the Communists in possession of mainland China and Chiang and the remnants of his forces seeking refuge in Formosa, 100 miles off China's southeast coast.

The historical background of these hot springs kept coursing through my mind. And as I climbed a winding staircase to the top of a short tower graced by a colorful pagoda roof, Mr. Yen, my interpreter, reminded me that the Queen had gone here to dry her hair after her baths, and that here, too, had been Chiang Kai-shek in happier moments and years.

As we enjoyed the hot sun mellowed by a cool breeze, Mr. Yen pointed below us to a colorful marble-floored stage where dancing girls once performed for the Queen. Now there are no dancing girls and the shaded walks and arched bridges that once knew no more than the patter of the clove-shaped, bound feet of a queen, now resound to the footsteps of thousands who can view the glories of the past for a few cents. For another few cents they can relax in hot spring baths once used by members of the Queen's court, but they are not allowed to use the Queen's own bath. That is kept under lock and key for the enjoyment of foreign visitors and party and government V.I.P.'s.

Not much has changed in the last thousand years as far as the hot spring resort is concerned. There are more people tramping its beautiful settings, the water discharged from the baths still flows into a pond studded with lily pads and frequented by fish doing exactly what their ancestors hundreds of generations back did when Queen Yang Kuei Pei made her toilet here.

GATEWAY TO THE WEST

LANCHOW. If this were the story of a comparable area in Canada or the United States, it would most likely start with "out here where the west begins." Even the Chinese are acquiring the habit of referring to this city as the gateway to the west, for it is from here that China's new railway starts on its way through the vast expanses of Sinkiang and Inner Mongolia, and on to Russia.

Nowhere else in China are the signs of change quite as visible and as sharply defined. From the air, as we circled, seeking an opening in the huge loess hills that reach almost a mile into the sky, the construction scars on the face of Lanchow were clearly discernible, despite the swirls of loess dust that frequently almost obscured the landing strip itself. Lanchow lies nestled between huge mounds of the fertile soil which is so important to the economy of China. It hugs the twisting Yellow River over which there is, at present, only a single bridge to link two sprawling communities into one. This bridge, built half a century ago by a British firm and guaranteed for forty years, is a solid mass of humanity, donkeys, carts, and trucks, from dawn to dusk, such is the tempo of activity here. A second bridge is under construction farther up the river.

Vast patches of this city give the impression of having been fought over by opposing armies. They have been swept clear of the mud-brick hovels that occupied them for centuries and today they are twisted and torn barren lands, with here and there a lonely piece of mud wall still standing. This scorched land awaits only the arrival of engineers and equipment to be launched on its particular role in the first, or the second, or some other five-year plan.

Broad new roads are being constructed, straight as an arrow, without regard for historical thoroughfares. Such has been the speed of construction and the need for roads that in many places time has not been wasted in tearing down the trees that lie along the route. The road simply separates at these points and becomes one when the obstacle has been passed. Along the sides of these new roads, some not yet graveled, lie vast dumps of materials—wire, structural steel, lumber, kegs of nails and roofing material, bricks and tiles— some of it covered with tarpaulins, some of it still exposed to the weather. It is all carefully guarded by weary-looking, dust-covered soldiers, armed sometimes with carbines, sometimes with revolvers.

The city has increased in population almost four times since 1949, and all that is needed to give it a real wild-west appearance is a few cowboys and Indians. Perhaps the thousands of barefooted Chinese lads jauntily sitting astride their Mongolian ponies, to the sides of which are strapped water buckets, could be thought of as cowboys. And the color traditionally attributed to the North American Indian is perhaps supplied by a handful of Tibetans, casually strolling through the streets in their pork pie hats, their gaily colored blankets, and their sweeping skirts (worn by the men) that just barely touch the top of their knee-length leather boots. The Tibetans are unconcerned by the contrast they make with the drab blue-and-black cotton uniforms that make all Chinese look like public washroom attendants.

In yet another way, too, Lanchow is typical of frontier towns, and that is in the high cost of living by comparison with older communities. It is understandable that staples other than those grown in the area should be more expensive, since most of them have to be hauled by rail from Peking, a journey of fifty-four hours. On an average, living costs are 15 per cent higher and, according to officials here, this difference is compensated for by higher wages. Despite the high cost of transportation, food, which is the main concern of the Chinese, is still comparatively cheap. In the Lanchow Hotel a full-course Chinese meal can be obtained for 60 fen (24 cents Canadian). A barely satisfactory European-style meal runs close to $1 Canadian, perhaps because coffee alone (without milk, which is generally unobtainable) is the same price as an entire meal of Chinese food, 20 per cent higher than it is in Peking.

The increase in population is largely accounted for by the huge army of men doing construction work. It is estimated that more than 200,000 are so engaged and from the uproar at 5:15 A.M. every day, when they start out with their donkey-drawn carts, it sounds as if most of them pass by the hotel. The new streets, all being built with pick and shovel and a scraper (a blade drawn back and forth by two men), are about 150 feet wide, with lanes on either side for the slower traffic —carts, pedicabs, and bicycles. There is no evidence of any provision for water mains or sewers along these streets. Apparently the town planners assume that the Chinese will be content to carry on as they have for thousands of years— drawing their water by bucket from the silt-laden Yellow River if they happen to live near it, or from an open ditch through the city that carries water pumped from the river. For those not handy to these sources there are the donkey water-carriers or huge tubs carried on a cart which deliver water to centrally located tanks. Sewage is traditionally not a problem in China, and even under this new regime which has attempted to make the entire nation health-conscious, the Chinese still pursue the most elementary method of disposal.

The new population of Lanchow has been drawn from many parts of China—Shanghai, Peking, Nanking—but the huge influx has not created a crime problem. It is admitted that there are occasional cases of rape and theft, but there was the usual Chinese reluctance to provide actual figures. Crime is such a minor problem, they say, that the police force (again no figures available) is being reduced in line with a recent directive of the Communist party that the administrators must be reduced in number.

RAILWAY TO RUSSIA

LANCHOW. This city is the starting-point of a new railway link that is punching its way north 1,800 miles to the Russian border. A stretch of about 500 miles has been completed, some of it with forced labor—political prisoners who are persuaded through hard work that they really don't long for a return of the old days before 1949. The target date for completion of the line to link up with a short one the Russians are now building toward China is 1961. The new line will not only cut in half the distance by rail to Moscow and the European markets, but will also open up the province of Sinkiang, which contains enough untapped oil reserves to make China self-sufficient in gasoline, oil, and lubricants.

Whether the completion date is to be realized depends to a large extent on how quickly the Chinese engineers can overcome the problems involved. The line will pass through a diversity of terrain which would be challenging to any country's engineers. After crossing the Yellow River and the 10,000-foot Wuhsiaoling mountain pass, the railway passes over the grasslands, marshes, and alkaline flats of the Kansu Corridor, a lowland strip between two high mountain ranges. After skirting the edge of the Gobi Desert it will cross the marshes and lakes of the Turfan Basin, which lies below sea level, and rise again to cross the 13,000-foot snow-covered Tien Shan Mountains.

A particular challenge to their ingenuity is the fierce wind in a forty-mile stretch through the Ala Pass (the Mountain Mouth) in the Tien Shan Mountains which lie astride the Sino-Russian border. So far, the Chinese have found no method of coping with winds so strong that they are likely to sweep the trains off the tracks. The wind is always pouring through the mountain mouth but for two and three days at a time it blows steadily at close to 100 m.p.h. The same problem faces the Russians who have not yet come up with an answer. One solution being considered is the planting of trees as a windbreak. However, Chi Hieng Yu, chief engineer in charge of surveying and designing, says the problem is complicated by the fact that when the high velocity winds from the northwest subside (they blow during the winter months), they are replaced in the spring by equally fierce winds from the southeast. Little surveying has yet been done in the area and most of the knowledge of the high winds has been obtained from the natives of the area, the Mongolians, who build their homes half buried in the earth so they won't blow away. The Chinese have worked out a system of protection at stations in the area so that when high winds are forecast, whole trains can be stopped at the nearest station to sit out the danger period. The open stretches still pose a problem in a country where the few trees that now survive are permanently bent almost to the ground by the continuous blowing.

The new line will skirt the western boundary of the Gobi Desert, where water supplies are non-existent. The solution to this problem may be the use of diesel locomotives. An alternative being considered is the laying of water pipes along the route.

In the Kansu Corridor the engineers had to cope with the problem of sheet floods. During the summer, water from the melting snows pours down the mountains, inundating the flatlands below and breaking into scores of small rivers directly in the path of the rail route. Rather than build a bridge for each of these temporary rivers, perhaps a hundred of them, the Chinese, at the suggestion of their Russian advisers, constructed a system of ditches on the slope above the railway to divert the smaller streams into larger ones before they reached the level of the railway. The result was that only about thirty bridges were needed.

The problem of thousands of acres of alkaline soil had to be faced in the same area. White and powdery in cold weather, this soil becomes pasty in the spring and summer when the frost is coming out of the ground and offers no stable base for a railway line. This difficulty was overcome by resurfacing the land for some distance on either side of the tracks with thick layers of sand and pebbles. So far, this new surface has been unaffected by frost boils.

Another problem was at Tiloyen cliff, 590 feet high, in the Kulang Valley in Kansu province. Years of erosion and frequent earthquakes have shattered the body of the cliff in thousands of places with the result that the vibrations of a train running alongside it might cause serious accidents from falling boulders. One suggestion, which was discarded, was to cement the cracks; another was to remove the top rocks. Again on the suggestion of the Russians, the Chinese blew up the whole cliff by what the Russians describe as a "spray explosion." It took three months to dig a tunnel, curving up for 150 feet, in which the explosives were placed. Because of difficulties in ventilating the tunnel, the men could only work in ten-minute shifts. This method of disintegrating huge rock masses has also been used on other lines. In one instance, 330 tons of explosives were set off to remove hundreds of thousands of cubic yards of rocks and jagged peaks and dump them into a valley, saving an estimated four months of work.

Since the line passes through large stretches where there are not sufficient quantities of stone, sand, and lumber available, great use is being made of prefabricated materials. Four factories in Lanchow are manufacturing reinforced concrete piers, culverts, and abutments. At shops along the route, track sections are fixed to the ties before being sent forward for laying.

TOIL AND SWEAT

CHUNGKING. The sight of men and women used as beasts of burden strikes home more here than in any other part of this vast country, perhaps because this city is built on hills and therefore peculiarly ill-suited to the use of draft animals, even the sure-footed donkey. There is scarcely a level stretch of road. Even the banks of the Yangtze and the Kialing, which form a peninsula where they meet to provide the site for Chungking, slope so sharply that there is barely room for an inclined road which motor vehicles negotiate with some difficulty. It is Chungking's unusual topography, unlike that of any other Chinese city, which also rules out the use of the pedicab, the all-purpose vehicle without which the economy of China would surely falter. Not even the stout backs and muscular legs of the pedicab drivers could negotiate the streets of Chungking, but men and women, hitched to carts like animals, do and must struggle to move the goods required by the 2 million persons who inhabit this city.

Many of the homes cling to the hillsides, accessible only by almost perpendicular flights of steps. The houses themselves, unlike those of the flat cities of China, are built up three and four floors high, since that is the only direction in which there is space available. In the business streets the buildings are fairly substantial, with mortar fronts; but Chungking's millions live in tenement-like wood and bamboo shacks that seem to have been added to, one at a time, one on top of the other, as necessity dictated. In their search for living space, the people of Chungking have burrowed into the hillsides of solid rock. They have gone underground, living in caves under the sidewalks and roads where the only natural light they get is the light that filters down the brief staircases, and the staircases have to be covered at night lest some unwary pedestrian tumble into them.

In all this vast jungle of hills and valleys, where the earth is almost lost from sight in the clusters of dwellings, there is not a single animal to be seen. The Mongolian ponies, the braying donkeys, and the lean horses, all familiar sights of other Chinese cities, are missing. In their stead are women, some obviously pregnant, some in bare feet, many old, and some barely out of their teens. They struggle and sweat, pull and push, to perform the tasks reserved for animals in other places. Women, sometimes as many as six to a team, painfully inch their way up an inclined road, struggling under the weight of steel girders, in painful and depressing contrast to one of China's new liberation trucks (built at Changchun), speeding by with its horn blasting, carrying no more weight than that of half a dozen other workers who have hitched a ride.

Women at manual labor are a common sight in China. It is a sight that is to be expected if women are to indulge fully in the new-found freedom bestowed upon them by the Marriage Law of 1950 and by the trade union regulations, which require that women shall have equal opportunity to work and shall receive equal pay for equal labor. In many of the cities of China women operate street cars. In Peking one would occasionally find a woman mixing cement. In the factories they operate lathes and overhead cranes; in the mines they repair machinery and wiring. It is not uncommon to see a woman climbing hydro and telephone poles. In cities in the northwest, such as Lanchow, a familiar sight is that of women jogging along the streets, carrying two buckets of water attached to either end of a bamboo yoke, neatly balanced at an angle across one shoulder. Sometimes these carriers of water were of school age but for the most part their pepper-and-salt hair indicated years numbering fifty or more.

Women, of course, are a vital part of the agricultural scene in China and do their full share of farm chores, plowing, weeding, planting, threshing, or else they don't get as much to eat as the men. This is one of the blessings bestowed on women by the land reform, which took the land from the landlord and gave it to the peasants, male and female alike, in equal shares. Women, therefore, must contribute an equal share of labor.

The airport lies outside Chungking, and to get to the city requires negotiating a winding road that spirals the mountains in such a fashion that quite frequently it is possible to keep looking straight ahead and see just above you, where you have just been. All along the tortuous road, which was really a mud patch, gravel was being prepared for the roadway, and it was being broken into the proper size out of chunks torn from the mountainside by women. There they sat, at intervals all along the route, each to her own rockpile, patiently pounding rock with a hammer. Here and there the tiny, bound feet of one of China's older females peeped out from behind a rock on which the larger stones were held by one hand while the other beat them into a convenient shape and size for the new China's roads. As we descended in the direction of Chungking, the pattern of these rock piles unfolded. The work had begun at the bottom of the road, and the task of the rock breakers would be completed when they joined forces at the top. Toward the bottom there were no workers. The piles of gravel reposed at the side of the road, resplendent in their hand-made neatness, mute monuments to a new concept of the dignity of man.

There are 10,000 men and women working as porters in Chungking. The expression "porter" is the Communist substitute for the despised expression "coolie," which has on it the curse of having been coined in the days before the 1949 revolution. A strong male porter (there was no mention of the weaker ones) averages 60 yuan a month ($24 Canadian) for which he labors eight hours a day, six days a week. Females, because in most cases they are wives and sisters of the male porters, and because "they are not very strong," as it was carefully explained to me, average 30 yuan monthly ($12 Canadian). There was no explanation of the differential in pay when women and men are hitched side by side to a wagon—a frequent sight.

All this degradation seemed to be symbolized in a scene I watched from the hotel doorway on a morning when it was raining more heavily than is normal in Chungking. The street running past the hotel is the Ming Shen Road, the People's Road, and it gradually inclines to the west. As I looked toward the intersection, a couple of Chinese were struggling to pull a loaded wagon across. One of them, an older man, was pulling on the handles and pushing his body against a canvas strap tight against one shoulder. His companion was a woman, probably about thirty, also hitched to the wagon, but to one side. I watched them struggle, inch by inch, sometimes bent until their faces almost touched the pavement. At times the weight of the load stopped their feet in mid-air and it seemed as if the wagon would pull away from them and roll back down the incline. Half way through the intersection, the old man dropped the load and thrust one foot under a wheel to keep it from pulling back; the woman unhitched herself and went behind the wagon. They got the vehicle rolling again, but with some difficulty.

As they inched their way out of sight, I turned to the half-dozen young, able-bodied, Chinese lads who apparently work in the hotel but never seem to do anything. They were paying no attention. At this point I couldn't help but recall the fatuous comment of the correspondent for an English news service in Peking that "at least here you don't see women having to do the work they do in Hong Kong."

ARCHITECTURE UNDER FIRE

CHUNGKING. Nowhere in China is there a better example than in this city of the kind of waste of public money the country's government is currently attempting to stem through a widely publicized economy campaign. Here, in China's wartime capital, is the People's Auditorium, a magnificent edifice, patterned on Peking's T'ien T'an, the Temple of Heaven, which was once the temple where the emperors of the Ming and Ch'ing dynasties made sacrifices to heaven. The auditorium cost the people of China more than 3 million yuan (more than $1¼ million Canadian) to erect, in the shadow of the nondescript building that served as headquarters for the Chiang Kai-shek government during the years of war with Japan. The auditorium is round, in accordance with the ancient Chinese astronomical conception that the sky was round and the earth was square.

Where the auditorium now sits was once a hill of rock. For six months the workers of Chungking worried away at the rock with their picks and their hands and carted the debris away in wicker baskets strung from a yoke thrown across one shoulder. Another three years were to pass before the auditorium was completed and beautifully landscaped on a site which measures about 160,000 square feet. A graceful gate permits entry to a long promenade, bordered by colorful flowers and bushes and trees, leading to a series of steps by which the entrance to the auditorium is reached. Inside is a true reflection of the color of Chinese architecture. High up, close to 200 feet above the floor level, are a ponderous dome and four balconies spread in a half-circle before a stage. The stage is graced by pale blue curtains on which are focused banks of spotlights.

There is room for 4,500 people to gather on any one occasion, and Mr. Kung, my interpreter, said the auditorium is probably used about ninety days out of every year—this, in a city with a population of more than 2 million. Its use? Mr. Kung shrugged his shoulders and recalled that a number of important government pronouncements had been made from the stage. It is available, too, if the women's organizations want to use it. Movies? Opera? No, just for important occasions involving personalities.

Later, over a dish of ice cream in a tea house in the People's Cultural Palace, a sort of city park and zoo combined, we got to discussing the People's Auditorium. I ventured the suggestion that the money used in erecting the auditorium would have provided a good many homes for workers. From Mr. Kung came that sharp intake of breath, so typical of the Chinese when they are faced with a difficult question. "It is estimated a factory could have been built for the same money," Mr. Kung finally replied.

In northeast China, in Harbin, is another example of what Li Fu-chun, China's vice-premier, has deplored as a waste caused by blind adoption of a so-called "national style"—undue emphasis on extravagant façades and decorations. In that instance it is a Communist party building in which costly or special materials have been used without regard for the principles of suitability, economy, and attractiveness. It has its broad towering roof, in the Peking fashion, at the price of a third of the entire cost of the building. Many instances of such waste are given by Mr. Li. There is the Changchun Institute of Geology, which he describes as the so-called "Geological Palace" and cites as a notorious example of extravagant building. As I mentioned in an earlier story from Changchun, the institute is built on the unfinished imperial palace the Japanese were building in the puppet state of Manchuria. Because of unnecessary decoration, the building cost 140 per cent more than the state-fixed ceiling cost. Without naming the building, Mr. Li also singled out a Peking structure where excessive ornamentation not only greatly increased building costs but reduced the usable floor space. In this instance, he said, the usable floor space is only 44 per cent of the total floor space of the hall.

Mr. Li also takes a rap at the excessive cost of some of the workers' housing projects. At the Anshan iron and steel works, housing was erected at a cost per unit of 163 yuan, as compared with an average cost fixed by the government at 125 yuan.

The cost of the general designing office of the Anshan iron and steel works was 60 per cent above budget, a waste, according to Mr. Li, of 1,380,000 yuan ($552,000 Canadian), and its usable floor space is less than 50 per cent of the total floor space of the building. He added that the cost of the laundry of a certain sanitarium was more than double the estimated cost, and that, after the installation of the laundry machinery, the space left over was so small as to cause great inconvenience to the workers. The kitchen cost almost double the estimate but has no room for storing rice and flour.

Such extravagant buildings which lay too much stress on form inevitably ignore the needs and interests of the people who use them, says Mr. Li.

RUSSIAN MOVIE

CHUNGKING. Since there is nothing else to do on a Sunday night in China (or any other night of the week for that matter), I readily agreed to the suggestion of my current interpreter, Kung Ling Wu, that we take in a movie. There are only twenty movie houses in Chungking for a population of more than 2 million. It is necessary, then, to order tickets in advance to be sure of getting seats, and at a slight hint from Mr. Kung I coughed up the necessary 30 fen (12 cents Canadian). It was well, as it turned out, that Mr. Kung had taken the precaution of booking seats. The theater, a post-revolution addition to the skyline of Chungking, seats about 900. Those unfortunates who failed to secure tickets in advance were crammed into the aisles and the open spaces between sections of seats, on narrow, backless benches, with the result that they leaned forward on their elbows breathing down the necks of those immediately in front of them.

At the suggestion of Mr. Kung, we arrived at the theater well in advance of the scheduled starting time, twenty minutes early, in fact. We spent about half this time loitering outside with several thousand others, while Mr. Kung attempted, to the best of his ability, to tell me something of the plot in advance. The name of the feature picture, he said, was *The Murder Story*. It was a Russian film, with a Chinese sound strip dubbed in. The locale was France, during the Second World War. This promised to be really something. I had seen several Chinese films during the past weeks but this was to be my first opportunity to examine the Russian product as it had been altered by the Chinese sound experts. I must confess, too, that the prospect of Russians playing the parts of French and Germans and speaking Chinese, intrigued me. I couldn't help but think what my newspaper's movie reviewer could do with this opportunity.

To illustrate the points he was attempting to make about the story, Mr. Kung kept pointing to colored photographs in a show window of the theater, each with its caption in Chinese, and properly numbered in sequence. Mr. Kung isn't a professional interpreter. He is a member of the Bureau of Protocol, a rather vague Chinese institution, the function of which is, apparently, to care for the wants of foreigners where China Intourist has no office. Since Mr. Kung sees few English-speaking foreigners (I was his first charge so far this year), his command of my mother tongue left something to be desired. This, plus the fact that at least a hundred Chinese had

126

managed to elbow their way between myself and Mr. Kung and the window, resulted in me losing most of the translation, since Mr. Kung addressed himself to another Chinese in the mistaken impression that I was at his elbow.

When a bell rang, warning that the program was about to start, we found our way to our seats; they were on the side, but gave a good view of the screen. They lacked only the padding one becomes accustomed to in the soft Canadian life. All around me the Chinese were settled back munching away at popsicles, which were being peddled by two women shouting at the tops of their voices. The bell rang again and then there was a few minutes' wait before slides were flashed on the screen—notices of features that were coming up. As a diversion from these, there were commercials for eye lotion, ink, and fountain pens, and a reminder that a healthy Chinese is a live Chinese, courtesy of the propaganda department of the Bureau of the Ministry of Health. The lights faded, the curtains parted, and on the screen appeared, in color, brief scenes from a coming attraction which was also to be a Russian production. I gathered from Mr. Kung that it had something to do with scientists in a storm. This seemed to be borne out by numerous scenes, brief ones, of waves dashing against rocks; what appeared to be a sphere for underwater exploration; a gunboat scanning storm-tossed waters with its searchlights; and lastly, someone in a medical outfit wiping the sweat off his brow.

There then followed the newsreel showing spring in Tibet; Chinese officials bending to the plow in Inner Mongolia; a football match between China and Japan; a new automatic coal selector; and a dinner in honor of two fellow-traveling foreign poets. On the heels of the newsreel there came another slide depicting a boy on a bicycle. There was a groan from the audience and the lights went on. This, Mr. Kung explained, meant that the feature film hadn't yet arrived. It was still showing at some other movie house but would be along shortly. And so it was, fifteen minutes later.

For the brief résumé of the plot of the picture which follows I must, in all sincerity, give full credit to Mr. Kung. He translated as the picture unfolded, his murmured remarks enriched considerably by the fact that he had obviously consumed a quantity of garlic at his evening meal.

The story begins in Paris, in 1945, just after the end of the war. A gendarme patrolling the street is alerted by a gunshot. He asks three youths strolling arm in arm (remember this scene) where the shot was fired. They don't answer but he finds his way to 29 rue Dante where a woman is lying flat on her back, a revolver on the floor beside her. From here the story is in flashbacks as the woman lingers in hospital telling her story to a doctor, stopping only now and then to drink something through the spout of a tea pot.

It seems that this woman, an apache dancer in Paris, takes off when the Germans invade France and winds up at the old country inn where she was born and where her father still lives, but only just. He is ill in bed. She decides to stay in order to run the inn, and becomes involved with the partisans who are shown in various partisanlike activities such as shooting up German convoys, blowing up bridges and trains, and even bouncing iron pots off the heads of German officers. When the officers aren't looking, of course.

Now this woman has a husband and a son. The husband, a doctor, is separated from her and seems to have no other purpose in life but to provide the apartment in which the attempted murder and earlier scenes are cast. The son is a real stinker. He is rounded up by the Germans but, unlike other French youths, is not sent off to concentration camp. The mother's suspicions that all is not well with her boy seem to be confirmed when the son accidentally discovers the hiding

ABOVE. Beside a narrow-gauge railway in Fushun, two aged women and three young children squat together grubbing for coal, picking and sorting fragments. They are relatives of some 16,000 workers in one of the largest open-pit coal mines in the world.

RIGHT. Coking ovens are like giant milk bottles rising behind sprawling hodgepodge of workers' houses occupying every foot of ground at Fushun. Everything except the people is black from constant exposure to smoke.

LEFT. New homes for workers in Fushun are built of brick with tiled roofs, but kitchen stoves are still outdoors and primitive.

OPPOSITE TOP. Workers digging a drain at a machine-tool factory in Anshan. Picks and shovels and manpower are still the mainstay of construction work in Red China as are the cattie baskets, carried by the man at right, to move earth and rocks. BOTTOM. New hotel in Lanchow, typical of those constructed by the Reds in country's main cities. Same plan is used for most of them, with slight variations in landscaping because of local conditions.

LEFT. Home garden on outskirts of Anshan. Although all farms are now co-operatively owned and operated, small pieces of ground are still available for private growing.

LEFT. Water wheel on co-operative farm near Lanchow on Yellow River. Use of irrigation in this area is new and makes three crops a year possible.

BELOW. Open-air greenhouse near Lanchow, on co-operative farm. Constructed of mud, it is used to start tomato plants and leeks.

ABOVE. Pony and plow on co-operative farm near Lanchow. BELOW. Inflated pigskin rafts used on the Yellow River. One man can easily carry one of these on his back but it will support five on the water. In most parts of the upper reaches of the Yellow River these rafts are the sole form of transportation.

LEFT. Construction work on new oil refinery on outskirts of Lanchow. Cement is mixed by hand and hoisted aloft in pails for pouring into the forms.

BELOW. Small carts, filled and pushed by workers, used to carry fill for new bridge being constructed across the Yellow River at Lanchow.

ABOVE. Site of blasting operations in Yellow River at location of Sanmen Dam. After blasts, debris is carried in baskets to the truck which will transport it to a dump several miles downstream at a point where it will not block the river during the flood season.

RIGHT. A portion of the new road constructed from the railway line to the site of the Sanmen Dam on the Yellow River. The road twists and winds through hills of loess, the fertile yellow soil which gives the Yellow River its name.

LEFT. With a hammer and chisel a worker carefully chips out inscriptions left on the rocks of the Yellow River by generations of Chinese to whom the river was the sole commercial highway. Water will cover the area when the Sanmen Dam is completed.

BELOW. Archeological dig in the Yellow River valley at staging area for Sanmen Dam. Professors from the Academy of Science have discovered tombs dating back to the early eastern Chou dynasty, 700–600 B.C. In tomb were found two chariots, complete with skeletons of four horses. Dig is covered with bamboo matting, used by the Chinese for many purposes—temporary walls, sun shades, rain coats, and to enclose buildings being demolished.

place of a partisan and when, in a subsequent surprise search, the Germans go directly to this place. Mother pops off to Paris to find that the boy is living with his father, and his room would seem to indicate that he is not exactly a normal French boy. Pornographic pictures line the walls and such trappings as boxing gloves, whips, and brass knuckles adorn his desk.

Mother's theater agent (and secret lover) is ambushed by the Germans and her boy Charlie (that's what she called him only she pronounced it "Sharlie") is seen at the scene, so mother goes back to the father for an explanation. Father merely gestures again to the boy's room. Now the décor is different. It is cluttered up with vacuum cleaners (dust cleaners, Mr. Kung whispered to me), the point of which escaped me.

The upshot of the story is that the mother suspects the truth and accuses her son. He threatens to shoot her when she suggests he give himself up but he cannot pull the trigger. The job is done for him by two hoods (also German collaborators) who had been listening at the keyhole. These two and the son are the three accosted by the gendarme, if you remember that far back and if you are still with me. A surprise switch is that the doctor who has been listening to this story is also a collaborator, and he gives the son and his two pals their comeuppance right across their mouths for having botched the job and not killed her. She dies, anyhow.

Then we see Charlie, after the war, with a newly acquired mustache, despite which he is recognized by a former partisan. When asked if he knows who did in his mother, Charlie says quite vehemently that he doesn't but he wishes he did. "So you're a Communist now," Charlie says to the ex-partisan. "Yes," comes the solemn reply, "and the future of France is safe with us."

Thus the fadeout, which prompts this final comment. The costumer, for all his care to see that the Russians truly represented the people they were portraying, apparently forgot that bell-bottomed pants were not worn in those days by the French.

THE CHUNGKING COCKROACH

CHUNGKING. The new China is fond of proclaiming that the proof of its patriotic health movement is in the absence of flies from its market places. There is a certain amount of truth in this claim, give or take a few million flies, but only if you don't stray away from Peking. The capital's flyswatters wage constant war on the flies and mosquitoes. In other parts of China the plain, ordinary, common housefly seems to be holding his own very well, along with the mosquito. Here in Chungking, these two pests have a particularly virile companion—the cockroach.

Now, I was no stranger to the Chinese cockroach. It is a sad fact that for all their newness, China's tourist hotels are all infested by this obnoxious insect. Even the newest hostelry, the Chien Men in Peking, still not landscaped, has acquired its fair share of cockroaches, almost suggesting that they came along as an integral part of the plumbing. The foreigner learns to live with the cockroach since its activities are nocturnal and few foreigners find occasion to be roaming around their rooms much after 10 or 11 at night. As a matter of fact, I should have been disturbed had there not been a few cockroaches on hand as a diversion on those frequent occasions when the radio gives forth nothing but Chinese opera (best appreciated in small doses) and everything in English has been read and re-read until it can be recited backward. So it was that I learned to respect the privacy of these little black friends as they scuttled for the open drain (with which all bathroom floors are equipped in China) every time I switched on the bathroom lights. I was aware of their presence but not to the point where any hostility seemed required, not, that is, until I arrived here.

For all my experience with Chinese cockroaches, I was not prepared for the spectacle that greeted me when I opened the door of my bathroom about 11:00 P.M., after returning from the movies. My eyes first fell on half a dozen black roaches, small ones, just like the little fellow that is crawling up the wall in front of me while this is being written. (A brief pause while the flat side of a book—Mao Tse-tung on New Democracy—is applied at the appropriate angle.) At first glance there seemed to be nothing out of the ordinary taking place in the bathroom. It was an ominous rustling that drew my attention to a wicker basket directly under the water tank of the toilet. Unsuspecting, I peered into it and there were six of the biggest cockroaches it has been my unhappy lot to meet anywhere in the world. I'm not entirely certain they *were* cockroaches, but since a couple of them made a beeline for the drain (when I gave the basket a hefty kick), I can only assume that a cockroach is known by the company it keeps and these disappeared into the same hole as the black ones of previous acquaintanceship. These new ones were outstanding specimens of some branch of insect life. They measured an inch and a half in length, as I ascertained later, appeared to be a pale red in the electric light, and were each equipped with two feelers which were forever searching the atmosphere about them.

All of this I had a chance to take in during the brief period while I stood watching them running frantically in circles around between the wall and the bathtub after the well-aimed kick at the basket had spilled them on the floor. Then I beat a hasty retreat to the sitting room, not forgetting to slam the bathroom door and snap out the light, assuming that once in darkness, the cockroaches would find their way back to their home in the drain pipe. As I perched on the edge of a chair, contemplating what strategy to adopt, my eyes fell on a small table across the room on the top of which reposed a jug of boiled water and a vacuum bottle of hot water. There, feeling its way around the bottom of the jug, was another of my new-found friends. The next step was unplanned. I bolted through the door and into the corridor to seek help.

Unable to locate the floor serviceman and not desirous of spending the night roaming the corridor, I ventured back into the room where the cockroach on the table top was still blindly seeking his way into the water jug. My strategy was obvious, even if improvised. Kill them, or scare them away. I decided to tackle the bathroom first. Switching on the light disclosed that all but one of these red monsters had returned to the basket. The remaining one I dispatched with my foot, not without some fancy stepping—he was speedy and I was wearing open-toed sandals, without socks, a concession to personal comfort dictated by the tropical weather that prevails in this part of China. It was this one that provided the carcass for gauging the average size of these new companions. The others, after considerable urging, found their way to the drain pipe, and I promptly covered the top with a wad of wet paper. I must confess that I attacked the one on the table with a flaming torch made of tightly rolled paper, since I was repelled at the idea of actually killing it on the top of the table. It disappeared in a hurry, seemingly under the table, and never showed itself again.

A painstaking examination of the bedroom, including the bed and the covers, revealed two more cockroaches, one half-hidden in a crack in the door jamb and the other trying to burrow its way into a corner of the clothes closet. The sharp corner of one of the new China's clothes hangers disposed of these remnants of the forces. And so to bed, after carefully closing both doors and sealing the openings at the floor with towels.

After a night that was not entirely free from tossing and turning I casually asked Mr. Kung, my interpreter, if he was aware of the presence in the hotel of some unregistered guests. The expression "cockroach" meant nothing to him. When I explained it was something like a beetle, only bigger and more loathsome, he still did not get it. I marched him upstairs and into my quarters to show him the evidence still reposing on the bathroom floor. "Oh, those," he chuckled. "Sure, we have a lot of trouble with them in the kitchen."

I am thankful for the availability of hardboiled eggs in the shell which shall provide an adequate if somewhat dull diet until the steamer leaves for the trip down the Yangtze River to Hankow, during the course of which I shall undoubtedly become acquainted with other members of China's insect life.

DOWN THE YANGTZE

The depressing effect of Chungking was merely the culmination of a reaction that had been gradually gaining strength during the preceding weeks. Seeing men working like animals was nothing new; it goes on all over China. Perhaps it was the hitching of men and women as teams that suddenly triggered the reaction. My depression was not relieved by the final recollections of Chungking: the communal garbage dumps where the stinking debris was spread over the sidewalk and onto the road and where women squatted on their heels sorting through it with their bare hands; youngsters, not yet of school age, scurrying like rabbits on the streets to recover discarded cigaret ends—they salvaged the tobacco, still warm from the last drag, and dumped it into a carefully guarded pile to be taken home to their parents for remolding into cheap cigarets.

The leisurely trip down this historic Chinese river was the perfect antidote. Here, amid the grandeur of soaring mountains, the whisperings of the current as it grasped at the hull of our steamer, and the tiny pigmy-like figures of the farmers as they patiently tilled little market garden patches, no bigger than a green postage stamp from our point of observation, it was possible to indulge in nothing but tourist thoughts and tourist reactions.

It takes three days and two nights to make the river journey from Chungking to Hankow. The first day and a half of this are spent in the upper reaches of the river, where it rolls swiftly between huge rocky precipices, worn almost to mirror smoothness. The picture that unfolded as we drifted down the river, the steamer's engines working just sufficiently to keep it on a straight course, was that of the China so familiar in paintings and photographs. It was the China of green hills, with their tiny mosaics of terraced gardens; the China of towering mountains with occasionally a stray wisp of fleecy cloud seemingly detached from the main body and trapped in a lofty crevice. Here there was none of the brassy veneer of Peking; the Japanese- and Russian-inspired orderliness of northeast China; the dirt and smell of Sian; the feverish frontier activity of Lanchow.

On the Yangtze, heavily silt-laden like all China's rivers, life had been going on like this for thousands of years. In its swift rush to the eastern lowlands, the Yangtze passes through a narrow valley, formed by steep mountains, dotted here and there with small villages. These cling to the rocky sides, threatening at any moment to lose their grip and slide into

134

the churning muddy water. Occasionally, herds of goats made white splashes on the green of the mountainside. Sometimes they were accompanied by rusty-colored cows, grazing at an angle with a surefootedness that only countless generations could have instilled.

We stopped for five hours at night at Wan-hsien, a pause marked only by a torrential downpour that probably sounded all the worse because of its impact on the canvas-covered top deck. The deck drains were inadequate to handle the water flowing along the gutters, and for a few hectic moments the flood was six inches deep outside the cabin. After a 3:00 A.M. start we sailed for hours between the same towering mounds of rock, worn to a shiny smoothness in places by sudden bursts of water inspired by storms such as we had just experienced. The rain had also left its mark on the few cultivated areas, where deep gutters, thrusting through freshly planted soil, testified to the ferocity of uncontained water.

It was about 8:00 A.M. when we entered the gorge area where the river picks up speed and narrows so much that only one steamer can negotiate it at a time. This sudden choking did not deter the boatmen who were going upstream; they could be seen feeling their way, clinging to the sides of the river where the current presumably is not as fierce. Where the terrain permitted, the crews jumped out on shore to pull the small craft upstream with a long rope. Where this was not possible, bamboo poles equipped with hooks were thrust into cracks in the granite sides of the mountains, to gain a few inches on the river dragging at the boat's bottom.

It is in this area that man is planning to make the first attempt to harness a river in the valley of which close to 300 million people live, and which handles 75 per cent of China's total river and sea tonnage. The plan is to erect huge flood-control dams on the site of the Three Gorges, one immediately following the other, where the river is at its narrowest. These will create an artificial lake reaching as far upstream as Chungking, provide water for irrigation and for electricity, and, what is more important, remove the ever-present fear of flooding which makes life hazardous for the millions living in the lower reaches.

For the present, at least, this portion of the Yangtze is the stuff of which prizewinning novels are made. The only indication that Communism has moved in is the occasional five-pointed red star implanted on the sparkling white façade of a building, looking for all the world like a Texaco gasoline sign at home rather than the standard of totalitarianism.

As the hours slipped away, so the mountains gave way to low, rounded hills. After an overnight run, the river had eluded the grasp of the highlands and we steamed through flat table-land, protected by earth dikes which gradually gained in height until only the thatched rooftops of the peasants' mud homes peeped above them.

THREE CITIES IN ONE

WUHAN. This country's government has amalgamated a group of municipalities for much the same reasons as prompted similar moves in other countries. However, one advantage this regime has over the governments of democratic countries is that it can order unification and, presto, it comes about. There is no reluctance on the part of anybody.

The name Wuhan appears at the head of this story, but it might have been Hankow, Hanyang, or Wuchang. These are the three municipalities which are now one, ranking within the first half-dozen cities of China as to population. Obviously the name of the new municipality is a composite of the three names. The three municipalities are separated by two rivers, the Yangtze and the Han. Hankow and Hanyang are along the north bank of the Yangtze and are divided by the Han. Wuchang is south of the Yangtze. Until recent years the only means of communication among the municipalities was the ferryboat. A railway bridge and a highway bridge now join Hanyang and Hankow, but Wuchang will continue to be relatively isolated until the completion of a two-decker, high-level bridge across the Yangtze.

The search for the reason for amalgamation of the three municipalities, and the results, led to a Mrs. Chang, identified as secretary-general of the People's Council of Wuhan. The difficult task of conducting an interview through an interpreter was further complicated by an interpreter who knew little more English than I do Chinese, and by the constant presence and interruptions of a pompous young representative of the Chinese Foreign Office, a Mr. Yang. The man from the Foreign Office, however, spoke fairly good English. He wrote down every question and answer, with many flourishes of his pen, and invariably started the answer with, "Before liberation, that is to say, in 1949. . . ."

Mrs. Chang, who might have been in her late thirties, was not any great mine of information, since she had been in her job for only about a year. She was, however, quite eloquent on the alleged evils of the Kuomintang regime. One of the great sins of the former government, Mrs. Chang said, was that it had prevented the amalgamation of the area. This, she insisted, had been for its own selfish purposes. More money could be made by government members if the three municipalities were kept separate. Just how this separation operated to the benefit of the Kuomintang officials was never made clear. The Communists, once they had defeated the Kuomintang, Mrs. Chang related, lost no time joining the three municipalities, thus achieving something which had been attempted four times during the preceding 1,300 years but which had never lasted longer than ten years at a stretch. Prior to 1949, the last attempt at amalgamation was in 1929. The union survived for only five months. Economically, politically, and culturally, the three municipalities were as one, Mrs. Chang said. The division which had persisted over the centuries, aided by the physical separation provided by the two rivers, was purely artificial, for the monetary benefit of a few officials.

The question of whether the inhabitants of the areas affected had been given an opportunity to express an opinion on amalgamation brought forth the stock Communist reply to such queries: "The people demanded it, so we respected the wishes of the people." Since there seemed little likelihood of determining just how the wishes of the people were made known, the interview was directed into other channels.

The combined area now has a population of just over 2 million, about double that of the 1949 figure; of these $1\frac{1}{10}$ million live in Hankow, historically one of China's chief commercial ports. It was developed originally by the British following a few excursions by gunboat up the Yangtze, and as a result, it has more the atmosphere of a European city, perhaps like that of Hong Kong, than the Chinese appearance of cities further inland. Wuchang has a population of 700,000, and there are about 200,000 in Hanyang, which appears to have been the Cinderella of the trio. Before amalgamation, it had no streets, no lighting, no water system.

"By satisfying the long-cherished dream of the people of the three towns to get together, we have made possible unification of street building, water supply, sewage disposal, schools, hospitals and transportation," Mrs. Chang said. As proof of the benefits of area planning, Mrs. Chang offered statistics, all based on comparison with 1949: as against 29 miles of sewers in 1949, there are 115 miles (these include storm sewers which empty into the near-by lakes that provide the city's water supply; sewage empties directly into the Yangtze); 200 buses operating on 21 routes as against 14 on one route; 8 roads (no mileage available) in Hanyang, where there were none; 14 ferryboats as against 8 to carry cross-river traffic that runs close to 100,000 daily. By the end of 1958, Mrs. Chang said, trolley buses will be operating in the city. The unified administration has built and repaired 189 roads; installed about 300 miles of watermain, including Hanyang's first water system; built a chlorination plant to filter and purify the river water; repaired about 150 miles of dikes; built 27 hospitals containing 7,000 beds; and provided 330 health centers and clinics.

All these activities are financed by a method so simple and convenient as to make Canadian civic fathers sigh with envy. There is a system of land taxes which Mrs. Chang was unwilling or unable to explain. The bulk of the annual budget (90 million yuan, or $36 million, this year) is the profit from sundry municipally owned projects handed over to Wuhan as part of the spoils of the revolution. There are about sixty of these projects, including textile mills, tobacco firms, and small machine shops.

SENTIMENT AND ECONOMICS

WUHAN. One of the major tasks being undertaken by the Chinese government is the relocation of industry. New industrial centers are being established inland, closer to the sources of supply. As part of this program, Wuhan is envisioned as a great iron and steel city and the key to the eventual industrialization of the southwest portion of the country. The government is inclined to mix sentiment and economic shrewdness, but not to the detriment of the latter. So it is that the creation here of an industrial base is intended to support the Communist propaganda line that under the previous regime Hankow and its sister municipalities, Wuchang and Hanyang, were maintained as purely commercial centers for the benefit of the Kuomintang government and its foreign friends. Now the Communists are diligently implanting the belief that the area is only now coming into its own because of the 1949 revolution.

There is a historical background to the eagerness of the Communists to create a metropolis out of Wuhan. It was here, in Wuchang, that a Chinese secret society (financed by Chinese who had settled and prospered in the United States and southeast Asia) started a revolt against the Manchu dynasty. The leader of the society was the late Dr. Sun Yat-sen, who was in Japan awaiting the call to form a new government in China. The revolt could reasonably have been expected to fail, but it was startlingly successful. It was the signal for the collapse in city after city of the worn-out imperial administration, and China became a republic. Although the Kuomintang, the immediate predecessors of the Communists, were organized by Dr. Sun, it was not he, but Chiang Kai-shek, who threw the Communists out and battled them for almost a quarter-century. The Communists, therefore, are not loath to call upon the spirit of Dr. Sun to support them in some of their theories, and here, as wherever else the opportunity presents itself, they have erected statues to his memory.

Two projects are now under way toward the fulfillment of the Communist dream of creating an industrial center out of an area that for centuries has lived on the trade along the Yangtze. One is the high-level bridge across the Yangtze, which will not only link Wuchang with Hanyang and Hankow, but for the first time in the history of China make possible a through train trip from Canton to Peking. In addition to being China's largest and busiest river, the Yangtze also successfully severs the most productive part of China, the south, from the rest of the country. Until the bridge is completed, sometime in October, trains will continue to be broken up at Wuchang, ferried across the Yangtze, and reassembled in Hankow. Passengers simply move by ferry to coaches on the other side of the river.

The bridge is undoubtedly the most widely publicized bridge in China. The Communists have printed thousands of words about it during the period of construction, and the odds are that it is being rushed to completion now so that it can be opened on October 1 this year, thus to play its proper role in the festivities of a day which Communist China now observes as its birthday. October 1 is National Day here, the start of a two-day public holiday, and marks the proclamation in 1949 of the People's Government.

The bridge is probably the most expensive single project now under way in China. It will cost, I was told, 130 million yuan ($52 million). This figure not only includes the structure but its approaches and a new railway spur. A double-decker, the bridge will carry rail traffic on the lower level and vehicles on the upper. Pedestrian lanes are being provided at both levels, on catwalks strung along both sides. The span's over-all length is 5,600 feet, including approaches. The steel portion is about 3,000 feet, and into its construction have gone 32,000 tons of steel and 5 million cubic feet of cement. To link the railway with the bridge it was necessary to construct ten other smaller bridges over Wuhan streets. As with all China's major construction projects, it was necessary to provide housing for the workers. Adjacent to the bridge site is a huge housing area with a population of 20,000, plus temporary schools, health clinics, and five public dining rooms. At peak of construction 12,000 were employed.

These statistics were supplied by Yu Chang Tung, chief of the office of the bridge, who was particularly proud of the fact that the Chinese engineers faced an unusual problem and mastered it, with help from Russian advisers.

At this point the Yangtze is normally 130 feet deep, so it was impractical to build the piers underwater using pneumatic caissons. The pressure would have been too great except during February and March when the river is at its lowest level. This would have meant taking four years to build the eight piers. At the suggestion of their Russian advisers, the Chinese used a new method, which consisted of driving reinforced concrete tubes, about five feet in diameter, to the rock bottom, while a jet of compressed air forced away the water and river-bottom mud. A five-ton diesel-powered electric drill was then lowered into the empty tube to crush the rock inside it and sink the tube itself about three feet into the rock. After the broken stone had been removed with a suction dredger, the tube was filled with reinforced concrete.

Southeast, in the Wuchang area, is the site of another big project, an iron and steel works designed to equal in size the largest mills now located at Anshan in northeast China. The site is about ten miles from the Yangtze, and the trip by car was for the most part over roads which could be compared only to back-country roads in Canada during the spring thaw. At intervals, for some unexplained reason, there were short connecting links of two-lane concrete paving, but for most of the way we plunged and bucked our way through mud and over pit-holes that challenged the lasting power of the car's springs and axles. Our driver, like all Chinese drivers, kept a heavy foot on the accelerator, with disastrous results for the pedestrians who were unable to scamper out of the way in time. Frequently we could hear the howls of dismay of groups of pig-tailed young girls whose Sunday best was now overlaid with a haphazard pattern of mud.

Again, the first part of the project to be undertaken was the provision of housing, much of it the stereotyped three-story apartment buildings so common to the Chinese scene and some of it one-level brick buildings (to save structural steel). There are 70,000 persons involved in the building of these housing areas and the initial stages of the plant. With their families they total 100,000.

Rather than use valuable growing land for the project, the Chinese chose a hilly waste, and leveled it—a two-year job that involved 10,000 men and machinery. Had not such machinery as bulldozers and steam shovels been used, it would have taken 30,000 men ten years to do the job. Che Kwang Kwin, engineer in charge of the project, had for some reason estimated that the amount of earth and rock moved in the leveling process would have been sufficient to build a road from China to North America and back.

The steel plant, which will obtain its iron ore from a mine located about sixty miles east of here, is being built in two stages, and the first part, which will be outfitted with Russian equipment, is expected to be completed in 1961, when it will start to produce 1,500,000 tons of steel annually. This production is to be doubled when the second stage is completed in 1964.

FEEDING THE AVERAGE MAN

NANKING. According to Professor Sun Pen Wan, of the geography department of Nanking University, who has been doing research on social science and China's population problem, the population of mainland China now stands at 653 million, and it is increasing at the rate of 16,325,000 annually, just about the total population of Canada. The last census held in China was in 1953. It provided a fairly accurate count of heads. The total at that time was 601,930,000, so there has been an increase of about 50 million during the past three years. At that rate (the natural increase has jumped from 20 per 1,000 in 1953 to 25 per 1,000 as of now) the population will have reached, in nine years, the optimum figure for the amount of cultivable land now available. It was Professor Sun who estimated this spring that China can comfortably support a population of 800 million.

This ideal total would not seem out of the way if there were any evidence in China today that the population it already has is being adequately fed. However, my personal observations, based on statements by peasants on co-operative farms and by city dwellers, have convinced me that about 30 per cent of the Chinese now under Communist domination are not getting enough to eat. There is just not enough food to go around, but the Communist administration, in its desperate efforts to construct an industrial base almost overnight as it were, is taking the food out of the mouths of its people and exporting it to pay for imports of industrial machinery. That is just one reason why about 200 million Chinese are never quite able to satisfy their hunger. The country is desperately short of foodstuffs due to two additional factors over which the Communists are unable to exercise any control. Last year was a year of prolonged floods that sharply reduced the total food crop. This year promises to be the same—large sections of southern China, the granary of this country of rice eaters, are now lying under water. Another factor influencing food production is the attitude of the peasants. The Communist land reform program, imposed by bloodshed in many instances, may have redistributed the land, but not even the exhortations of Chairman Mao Tse-tung have been able to convince the peasants that they should work any harder for the new land-lord than they did for the old.

Perhaps a word of explanation is required here. The land reform, the chief appeal the Communists made to the peasants to gain their support prior to 1949, resulted in the land being taken from the landlords and given to the peasants. Every peasant, and in many instances his wife also, was allotted a piece of land and given a brand-new deed testifying to the new ownership. As the years rolled by, the peasants found that as the result of a quiet but steady economic pressure, it behooved them to throw in their lot with the state co-operatives, so that now probably about 97 per cent of the cultivated land in China is co-operatively farmed. There has never been any public acknowledgment by the Communists that the land is no longer privately owned; that in fact the deeds are not worth the paper they are printed on. Publicly the Communists maintain the fiction that a peasant voluntarily joins the co-operative and that he can secede from it at any time he so desires. Privately, however, government officials admit, it could be extremely difficult and not very practical for a peasant to revert to private farming. Human nature being what it is, in Red China as well as anywhere else, the peasants are dragging their feet. They do just enough to assure themselves of sufficient food. There is no incentive to produce more than they need, simply because much of the surplus will go to the government in any event, and because there are few consumer goods available for purchase which would inspire an extra effort.

As recently as June 26, Premier Chou En-lai, in a report to the fourth session of the first National People's Congress in Peking, admitted that the Chinese are not getting enough to eat. Here is what he had to say on the subject: "Since the liberation, as a result of land reform and the co-operative movement, 20 to 30 per cent of our peasants today have a little more than enough, about 60 per cent make an adequate living, and 10 to 15 per cent are short of food and clothes." If due allowance is made for the possibility that the Communists may be inclined to play down the real situation, it is not difficult to appreciate how a foreigner who has seen more of China than most Chinese will ever see can get the impression that a lot of people in this country are always hungry. I asked Professor Sun about this. I told him the estimate I had been given by many people in various parts of the country. "Is it a fact," I asked him, "that 30 per cent of the people of China do not actually get enough to eat?" Professor Sun, a roly-poly fellow, wearing steel-rimmed glasses, was already perspiring profusely. He wiped at his neck with his handkerchief, jerked his head a couple of times, and replied: "On the average, everybody in China gets enough to eat." I protested: "But, Professor Sun, you can't average stomachs." He repeated it. On the average everybody in China gets enough to eat.

THE CHRISTIAN CHURCH

NANKING. It is difficult for a foreigner to assess the place of the Christian church in Red China. On the surface it would appear that a rather comfortable truce has been arrived at between the forces of Christianity and the members of a Communist regime who quite candidly admit they are atheists.

The constitution of Communist China, adopted June 14, 1954, provides for freedom of speech, freedom of the press, freedom of assembly, association, procession, and demonstration, and freedom of religious belief. From my own observations, there is no interference by the regime with Christians going to church to worship. During the ten weeks I have been in this country, I have visited dozens of churches—Roman Catholic and Protestant—when services were in progress. Except for the fact that the congregations were all Chinese, they might have been worshipping in any part of Canada. None of the services was crowded. It is estimated there are fewer than 4 million Christians in mainland China. About 3 million of these are Catholics, and of approximately 800,000 Protestants perhaps 100,000 are Anglicans. The remainder are adherents of the Presbyterian, Baptist, Methodist, Lutheran, Congregational, Pentecostal, Apostolic Faith, Seventh Day Adventist, and other denominations.

When I was in Chungking, it was my privilege to wander into a beautiful old ivy-covered Catholic church where evening mass was being said. It was raining heavily, as it had been for some days, and it was a heart-warming sight to see Chinese mothers and their children making their way through the driving rain to the church door. I stood outside for about five minutes. As I listened to the clear, pure voices of the children, doing their chanting in Chinese, paced by a heavier voice in the same language, a little fellow of not more than five years toddled up to the door. He was protected from the rain by a bright, yellow parasol. He paid not the slightest attention to the foreigner who was half blocking the church door. He neatly shook the rain off the umbrella, collapsed it, wiped his feet carefully on the mat, and tiptoed in.

I was hesitant to penetrate far into the church, not that there would have been any attempt to stop me, but that I had been cautioned weeks before in Peking that surprise visits to churches, Catholic in particular, might prove embarrassing to the minister or priest. For this reason I made no attempt to locate the priest but stayed merely long enough to observe the congregation. There were perhaps about 150, most of them children and the rest women, with the exception of three men who appeared to be in their late twenties.

I had discovered the church quite by accident when I was exploring the city on my own, much to the annoyance of my interpreter who was sure I would lose myself. Later I attempted to make contact with the priest through official channels. The first reaction of the interpreter was that he knew nothing about the church. He did not even know its name and since there was nothing in English to identify it I do not know its name yet. At my insistence the interpreter promised to arrange an interview. I left Chungking two days later without anything further having been done about the request.

When I reached Nanking I asked for and was granted permission to see Rt. Rev. Ting Kuanghsun, Bishop of the Chung Hua Sheng Kung Hai, which is the Anglican Church of China, and dean of the Nanking Union Theological Seminary. As secretary of the World's Student Christian Federation from 1948–51 he visited universities and churches in the United States, Canada, Latin America, and Europe. During that period he lived in my home city, Toronto, for several months.

Bishop Ting speaks excellent English as does his charming wife, who sat in on the evening interview in their home. The interpreter, at his own suggestion, gracefully bowed his way out and spent the next two and a half hours sitting in another room. Other than the fact that I was a foreign newspaperman, from a part of the world which is suspect to the Chinese Reds, there was no reason why a frank and honest discussion of the position of the Chinese church should not have taken place. After a few preliminary rounds during which I brought Bishop Ting and his wife up to date on developments in Toronto, I was able to pose the two questions that had been on the tip of my tongue for weeks. "Is there not something inherently incompatible between Christianity and Communism? How do the Chinese Christians reconcile their belief in God with the views of a governing group which does not believe in any God?"

There was not, Bishop Ting assured me, anything at all incompatible in the arrangement. It was only since the Communists seized power in China that the Chinese church had been able to free itself of foreign influence in the form of missionaries from abroad. The Chinese Christian church, the bishop insisted, is now purely Chinese. There are no foreign missionaries connected with it, and as a result of self-administration, self-support, and self-propagation, it is now truly stable and firmly rooted in Chinese soil.

The Chinese church does not feel there is any conflict between its teachings and the dogma of the Communist government, Bishop Ting told me. "As a matter of fact," he added, "our task is somewhat easier since the Communists frankly admit they are atheists. Not all Chinese have accepted Marxism, so there is a large area untouched by Marxism. I do not feel Marxism constitutes a threat to the church." Bishop Ting went on to explain that the Chinese church is going through a period of transition and adjustment in its thinking. "We are making our church Chinese but we are not against international relations with churches abroad," he assured me.

Somehow or other we got talking about "the people," the most common expression in the Communist vocabulary. I had to listen once again to a recital of the components of the people—the workers, the peasants, the petit bourgeois, the bourgeois, and the intellectuals. All others, Bishop Ting said, are enemies, who can be redeemed and restored to the ranks of the people by confessing their crimes. Turning to Mrs. Ting, I recalled some of the distressing scenes in the new China—men and women working as animals, for instance. Was this not distressing to Chinese Christians also? "But," she protested, "did you not notice that they are all wearing something on their feet? You would not have seen that before liberation." Mumbling something about being sure I had noticed some of these people in their bare feet, I politely bowed my way out, feeling somehow that I had once again listened to a record which has been played again and again during all these weeks in Red China.

When I reached Shanghai I continued my search for an explanation of the seeming incongruity of the Christian church continuing to function under a regime that is admittedly atheist.

Incidentally, before 1949, half of China's industry and business was concentrated in Shanghai, but now the city has all the appearance of having gone to seed. Most of its imposing skyscrapers—and they are imposing and unusual in mainland China—are now used as living quarters, easily identified by the personal laundry which flutters in most of the windows. The Communists' claims that Shanghai has regained its importance as a city of commerce are not borne out. There is an obvious lack of activity on the Whangpoo River, which provides a flowing border for the famed Shanghai Bund, this city's main business street. Where once more than 10,000 foreign ships berthed during a year, the best the Communists claim is 683 vessels last year. The city has an imposing new airport, glistening white. It has two levels, the upper a huge chamber held together by slender pillars. However, the day I arrived there were three people working in the lower level to handle my luggage, and the only sign of activity in the vast expanse of the upper waiting room were seven Chinese grouped together, busily playing cards.

The pursuit of the truth about Chinese Christianity involved a tour of four churches and a two-hour conference with five church leaders, including two bishops. I was accompanied by a group of New Zealanders and Australians. Two of them were ministers and they did most of the questioning. The delegation from Down Under were in China as invited guests of the government. They had come from Singapore where they

150

had been attending the world peace conference. My associates in the mass interview were: Rev. A. M. Dickie, from a Presbyterian church in North Essendon, Victoria, Australia; Rev. E. J. O'Rourke, a Presbyterian minister from Perth; Jack Metcalfe, a church student-leader in Melbourne; George Smith, president of the Metal Sheet Workers' Union in Melbourne; and Mrs. Hilda N. Parry, national secretary of the New Zealand Peace Council. Answering the questions were: Bishop K. T. Mao of the Anglican diocese of Kiangsu province; Pastor Chi, chairman of the Baptist Convention; Bishop Z. T. Kaung of the Methodist Church in China; Rev. K. T. Wu, also a Methodist minister and chairman of the National Christian Council; Mr. Sun, a Methodist minister; Y. C. Tu, general secretary of the Y.M.C.A., and Dr. H. H. Tsui, general secretary of the Church of Christ in China.

The interview, in a pleasant, comfortable room equipped with soft, leather-covered furniture, and enhanced by large quantities of sandwiches, sweets, and tea, began with a question by Mr. O'Rourke as to whether the Church of Christ was a national church of China or an amalgamation of several groups. It is a united church, Dr. Tsui replied, comprising missions operated by the following: the Presbyterian, Baptist, and Congregationalist churches of England, Ireland, Scotland, New Zealand, and Australia; the London Missionary Society; the United Church of Canada; the Reformed United States Church and the Reformed Church in the United States of America; the North and the South Presbyterian Churches of the United States of America; the United Brethren; and the Swedish Mission. This united church has seventeen synods, a membership of 120,000, and its own system of government. It is not a national church, Dr. Tsui assured us.

At this point the answering was assumed by Mr. Tu, the Y.M.C.A. secretary, who was spokesman for most of the remaining time we spent with the Chinese ministers. Mr. Tu assured us there is no movement in China for a national church. "Nobody even talks about it," he said. What is happening, he indicated, is that each denomination is free to arrange its own affairs and develop in whatever way it considers proper. "While we fundamentally believe in Jesus Christ, in matters of tradition, government, creed, methods of worship, we go our own ways." There is, however, an increasing degree of co-operation among the Chinese Christian churches, Mr. Tu continued, especially in evangelistic programs and theological seminaries. "The churches are coming together more closely. Before liberation this was not possible because of the existence of mission boards. We have been taught a great lesson and now fully appreciate the value of co-operation with one another in real Christian fellowship."

Mr. Tu agreed when asked by Mr. O'Rourke if in mainland China the Salvation Army is permitted to parade with a band in the streets but may not conduct open air services. He said the same rule applies to all Chinese churches. "Then how," asked Mr. O'Rourke, "do you conduct evangelistic campaigns if you cannot preach in the open?" "We have plenty of church space available for that kind of work," replied Mr. Tu, indicating what he meant with a wide sweep of his cigaret holder. The holding of open air meetings or street preaching is not a problem at this time: "In the old days we could find a lot of people who had nothing to do. These days there are very few people who would have the time to stop and listen for even half an hour, if you started preaching." The guarantee of freedom of worship also complicates the evangelistic work, Mr. Tu said. "In the old days we could go, for instance, to a Buddhist temple and condemn them to their faces. Not any more, and if you preached on the streets now there might be some atheists in the crowd. A street row would start and we would be endangering public safety."

The appeal of the Chinese church must now be on a purely religious basis, Mr. Tu explained. "People will now join the church because they feel a certain religious need. From the long point of view, our job should be easier because we are presenting a message pure and simple. We can only present Jesus Christ. There are no other strings attached."

"In another way," Mr. Tu said, "we are faced with a challenge. The old ways of preaching have lost their value because our country has been developing rather fast." Mr. O'Rourke asked if he agreed that the Chinese need a spiritual balance to the increasing worship of material things. "We need a more positive message," Mr. Tu replied. "I don't say the present society is free of evil but the old days were full of evils—opium smoking, widespread prostitution, corruption, squeezing, robbery, gambling, criminal behavior. Christianity had that to battle in the old days. It did make a contribution but it didn't solve such problems as opium smoking. These things continued to be. That is gone and so that kind of appeal is gone."

Mr. Smith, the Australian trade unionist, suggested that in thirty or forty years the Communist state will have taken the place of the church and that even today Chinese youth feel no need of the church. Bishop Kaung objected. "That is not a fair statement," said the Bishop, who added that he is seventy-three (seventy-four by Chinese count since children are considered to be a year old when they are born) and that he has been a Christian preacher for fifty years. "Our people are happy. They are looking forward to better days. I would think there would be room for gospel preaching. There is a future here for the church. There is a longing need for spiritual food which only Christianity can give."

As we filed out of the church building, following a brief prayer by Bishop Kaung in which he declared that in the eyes of God we were not Chinese and foreigners but simply human beings, I turned to Mr. Dickie with the simple question,

"What do you think?" His reply was: "At the moment there is undoubtedly freedom of worship. For the present the church does not constitute a threat to the Communists. It will in perhaps twenty or thirty years. Then there will be no more church."

PAINFUL HONESTY

PEKING. During the many weeks of travel in mainland China I was completely confident that my person and my belongings would remain inviolate. And so they had, confirming a blessed ease of mind which had had its origin in the first few minutes after penetrating the Bamboo Curtain so many weeks ago. The assurance given me that no one would tamper with my baggage in China had a genuine ring. I took the Chinese at their word and never had cause for regret. During the many thousands of miles I traveled on the mainland, by train, plane, boat, car, and pedicab, I treated my belongings with a careless abandon that would undoubtedly have been viewed in other countries as evidence of inexperience, and made me fair game for those bent on plundering the green traveler.

The only occasions on which I bothered to lock my bags were when they were in transit, and this precaution was taken because sad experience had indicated that Chinese porters simply do not appreciate the intent and purpose of "fragile" notices on bags and crates. It is a fearsome sight to witness the deliberate thoroughness with which the Chinese porters subject luggage to tortures undreamed of by the manufacturer. The size or strength of the package or bundle to be handled makes not the slightest difference. Heavy crates are seized and

154

tossed in on top of soft, fragile bags, without regard for the possibility that the bags might burst open under the impact of several hundred pounds of dead weight.

The porters' carelessness was painfully impressed on me during a frantic fifteen minutes in Peking airport where I was waiting to pick up my bags after a flight from Shenyang. Out of the hold of the plane came a tan bag, propelled in the direction of the cart. The bag struck one corner of the cart, took off into open space, and burst asunder, exposing its contents for all to see. The guffaw that was instinctively prompted by this misfortune was quickly choked off by the realization that it was my underwear and shirts that were being whipped nonchalantly across the airstrip by the breezes. My dismay was not lessened by the fact that the bag also contained several hundred Chinese yuan, left there simply because western pockets are not built to adjust themselves to thick wads of paper currency, the highest denomination of which is 5 yuan ($2 Canadian). With the eager assistance of about thirty Chinese who seemed to spring from nowhere, the bits of paper money and pieces of clothing, much of it the worse for having been dragged through the mud, were recovered. Since I had acquired the habit of keeping careful tab on the paper money not immediately required, I knew to the fen how much was in the bag; not a fen was missing.

I have told this story primarily to illustrate the almost painful honesty of the people of China. It is practically impossible to persuade them even to accept a tip, especially if they are employed by the government. The nearest approach to a tip was the acceptance, infrequently, by a waiter or a floor serviceman of a package of cigarets. Money they would not touch.

Another instance of the integrity of the people was given to me on one occasion when we stopped overnight along the Yangtze River. I bought a bamboo fan for 25 fen (10 cents

Canadian). I gave the woman 30 fen and walked away, busily brandishing the fan in a vain attempt to cool an atmosphere heated to an almost unbearable degree by about fifty Chinese children who were swarming about me as I strolled along the street. It was a good five minutes later when I turned my head in response to a swirl of activity behind me to find that the fan seller had followed me to return the 5 fen in change.

My faith in the honesty of the Chinese under Communist rule, bolstered by these and many other similar incidents, was understandably somewhat shaken when I discovered that my interpreter, Mr. Yen, did not share the same high opinion. The disclosure came when I rapped on his door one morning before breakfast. "Just a moment," he called. There followed a great rattling of a key and a bolt in the door and Mr. Yen poked his head out. I was somewhat shocked by the obvious precautions he had taken to ensure a privacy which I had been taking for granted (I had no key to my room and had never even considered asking for one), so I said: "Why do you lock your door? I thought all Chinese were honest." There was something of a sheepish look on Mr. Yen's face when he invited me in and replied: "Oh, not all the Chinese are honest. Perhaps only 90 per cent."

Until that moment, Mr. Yen and other interpreters and officials in China had vehemently rejected any suggestion on my part that the possibility of being shot had a lot to do with the reluctance of the Chinese to gamble or help themselves to articles left lying around. Having been caught in the act of bolting his door, Mr. Yen was so confused that he was willing to admit, in subsequent discussion, that fear of severe penalties was the main contributing factor in keeping the Chinese on the straight and narrow path. For a Chinese caught stealing from another Chinese, the penalty would depend on the severity of the theft, Mr. Yen explained. It could be a jail term or reform through labor, the Communist euphemism for slave labor.

"But what if he is caught stealing from a foreigner?" I asked.
"Is it possible he might be shot right here?" indicating the back
of my head with my finger. It was quite likely that that would
be the punishment, Mr. Yen sadly agreed.

THE SPITTOON'S LAST STAND

PEKING. For all the effectiveness of Communist propaganda
in convincing the Chinese people of the danger to health of
flies and mosquitoes, the regime has not yet been able to
convince them that spitting is an unhealthy habit. Spitting is
the favorite sport, indoors and out, of the Chinese, and it does
not take a stranger long to realize the folly of passing too
close to doorways or windows or to the open windows of buses
and street cars. Strolling down a street can be hazardous until
one learns to be on the alert for the traditional warning sound.
With the Chinese, spitting is no casual affair. It is a production,
which commences somewhere deep in the stomach and results
in what is known, in the language of the street, as a hawk.

This national habit, indulged in equally by women and men,
is the basis for what would appear to be a very profitable side-
line of the Communist regime—the manufacture of spittoons.
While it is difficult to secure exact figures, as it is in the case of
all other forms of production in mainland China, personal
observation would indicate that, judging by the extent to which
they are used, there must be about 300 million spittoons in
China. Spittoons are as important to the décor of a hotel room
as the bed or chairs or lamps. The lobbies of hotels and public
buildings are liberally splashed with gleaming white pots
equipped with long-handled wooden covers and looking for

all the world like rows of silent soldiers, standing at attention, waiting only the call to serve China's expectorating millions. So important is the spittoon in the scheme of things in China that caring for them is a full-time task to which youths of the new order conscientiously devote themselves. This is particularly noticeable on trains, where a spittoon is provided for every four seats, plus a few more strategically placed at the entrances to washstands and lavatories. One member of the train crew, proudly wearing a red arm-band, has the responsibility of seeing to it that the receptacles are prepared for the onslaught which will inevitably be visited upon them.

Of all the noises in China, and there are a multitude of them, the constant spitting, on the streets and indoors, is the one which seems to grate most on the ears. Hong Kong has more than 3 million Chinese inhabitants, but they are restrained from clearing their throats in public by signs warning of heavy fines. No such warnings are seen in China, so spitting is indulged in with an abandon and a frequency that makes a foreigner wince, particularly when the act takes place, as it frequently does, in the kitchen of a hotel and just at the moment when a fork of scrambled eggs is en route to one's mouth.

While not wishing to seem to be of a complaining nature, I discussed this subject frequently with my interpreter. He seemed not to have been aware of the intensity of the assault on one's ears and nervous system until I drew it to his attention. In the course of our discussion, I made him acquainted with the vernacular word for the act of spitting and I cannot recall his being more tickled than the night we were at the opera and I winced every time a member of the audience spat (as they did frequently), on both sides, behind, and in front of me. It was a hitherto unrevealed sense of humor in Mr. Yen that prompted him to nudge me with his elbow and whisper, with a half laugh: "That's a hawk."

Having thus enriched Mr. Yen's vocabulary, I proceeded to explore the situation with the Ministry of Health. "What about this deplorable, filthy habit of spitting?" I asked Dr. S. F. Chiang. The doctor seemed somewhat startled by the direct approach—it had been prompted by the unhappy fact that just a few minutes before I had forgotten to duck. "Yes," he admitted. "It is terrible." The problem, Dr. Chiang confessed, is what to do about it. Party members do not have spittoons in their offices or homes. Nevertheless, spitting is admittedly a national habit in China and, he assured me, it is recognized as a menace to health. There are, Dr. Chiang explained, basic historical reasons for the addiction of the mainland Chinese to clearing their throats in public. The habit was acquired centuries ago and was indulged in by poor and rich alike. The poor, because of constant ill health and inability to secure sufficient food, were easy prey to respiratory diseases and thus acquired the habit of spitting. The rich Chinese also acquired it. "In the old days a rich Chinese would never have to walk. He would be carried in a sedan chair. He became fat and soft and easily caught cold. So he, too, began to spit constantly."

Dr. Chiang then made the frank admission, for a Communist official, that his department had been unable to come up with a solution to the problem. "Not even now when everybody's health is so much better and everyone gets enough to eat can we persuade our people to drop the habit."

In a careless moment of levity I suggested: "Maybe if you shot a few people in the back of the head, spitting might suddenly become unpopular." The reaction was astonishing. Dr. Chiang jerked his head from me to the others in the room, none of whom understood English, then looked straight at me and said: "Ah, but we do not shoot people in China." Then he explained my suggestion to his companions and they burst into loud laughter. "That's a solution worth considering," Dr. Chiang conceded, with a half grin.

BEHIND THE MASK

PEKING. It is extremely difficult for a visitor to China not to acquire a deep affection for the Chinese. They are a lovable, hospitable people. These natural traits have lost none of their genuineness in eight years of totalitarian austerity which have induced a puritanical atmosphere that might well be envied by Oliver Cromwell if he could witness it. There is a monotonous sameness about the Chinese which is enhanced by the almost universal adoption of the shapeless uniform favored by Chairman Mao Tse-tung. The only variation is provided by the tunics and trousers which seem to be mismates simply because they have not faded equally in the many washings required by a government that rations cotton and urges its people to make one outfit last twice its normal life. This new look, which had its origin in the desire of party functionaries to emulate Mao, and perhaps to emphasize their own personal loyalty to the system being imposed on China, is now justified in the interests of national economy. It is much cheaper and simpler to grind out millions of garments, identical except for color and size, than to indulge in the expensive whims of those individuals who might not elect to be just faces in a huge, drab populace.

It is not only the cheap cotton garments which suggest that the people of Red China have been subjected to a physical readjustment so that all shall seem to be cast in one mold. There is a grim soberness on all the faces which tends initially to call for some caution in approaching the Chinese. The first impression is that these are a determined people and this reaction is carefully nurtured by the flood of propaganda which welcomes the new arrival to Red China. It would be so easy for a visitor to spend a few weeks in Communist China and emerge with stars in his eyes—Red stars, that is.

The sober, unsmiling attitude of the Chinese as they go

about their daily tasks is not, as the Communists would like to believe, outward evidence of an ideological evangelism, but rather a disinclination to be the first to ease the grim atmosphere. That this is so is immediately apparent when even the slightest overture of friendship is made. In any other country the simple act of grinning would be instinctive. Not so in China. It is almost as if the people disciplined themselves not to indulge in spontaneous displays of mirth. These, it would seem, must be reserved for the occasions when mass welcomes are laid on for visitors—when everybody will laugh on signal— and for the rare opportunities given the ordinary Chinese to visit the opera, watch a comedy movie, or gather on the streets to view the occasional traveling stage show. It is not difficult to appreciate how a nation can so completely abandon its inherent gaiety when its people are being constantly exhorted by their Communist leaders to cast off their old selves and take on new selves—to make a change, inside out. The Chinese are daily reminded in their newspapers and over Radio Peking that they are being trained as Socialist-minded, cultured, healthy working people. The Chinese, Premier Chou En-lai tells them, must not be frightened by any hardships they may have to face. They should make up their minds to overcome them and carry on honest labor. And they have Premier Chou's assurance that labor is the most glorious thing in mainland China.

There is no doubt that the Chinese have heeded the advice of their Communist masters, partially, at least. There has been a change outwardly, but it takes very little in the way of encouragement to make it quite evident that the grim determination of the new China is only a thin veneer. It is necessary only for a foreigner to make the first move, and if he makes it with a friendly smile, the response is all the more pleasing—an immediate wrinkling of the face in the shy grin so typical of the Chinese, regardless of age. The response of a crowd to such a simple friendly gesture as a smile is a heart-warming experience.

Smiling countenances burst forth with the speed of the sun breaking through storm clouds. Not even the trained functionaries of the government are immune.

Looking back at it, the game of cards played on a train between Chengchow and the Sanmen Gorge would have been a routine affair in any other country and at any other time. It was significant because it represented another successful attempt to break through the cold shell in which so many Chinese have enclosed themselves. It was a simple card game; the main purpose was to get rid of as many cards as possible. It might be familiar to Canadians as "crazy eights" or "snap." I suggested it and started to play it with my interpreter, who responded with a good many honest laughs. The interest shown by two Chinese neighbors prompted an invitation to participate, which they accepted. So we sat and played cards as the train rolled through the Yellow River valley, and one by one, silently at first and then gaily chattering, most of the rest of the car's occupants joined in as spectators. The warm chuckles elicited by a win and the firm pressure on my hand when it came time to break up the game were sufficient assurance that my Chinese companions, with whom I was unable to converse except through the interpreter, had thoroughly appreciated the opportunity to indulge briefly in a bit of fun.

NO DOGS IN CHINA

PEKING. About three weeks after my arrival in China, I woke one morning to the realization that in all that time I had not seen a dog nor heard a bird. The scarcity of birds was readily understandable. In a country of more than 650 million people, meat at a meal can only be acquired on rare occasions. The conclusion that there were no birds in Peking simply because the Chinese had eaten them seemed quite rational. But this hardly seemed an adequate explanation of why there was not a dog to be seen anywhere in the city.

Cats there were, by the thousands. Sleek and fat, almost the size of dogs in some instances, they made the nights hideous with backyard yowlings. Undoubtedly the hugeness of the cats was due, in great part, to an unrestricted diet of mice and rats, of which there seemed to be plenty. In the early morning hours when their alley symphonies made sleep impossible, the cats presented a fearsome sight, outlined by the moonlight, clinging to the ridge of the roof of a one-story dwelling across from the hotel.

I had by now reached a degree of understanding with Yen Pao-chiu, my interpreter. Our discussions of Communism were friendly, and he had reached a peaceful acceptance of my view that I wasn't at all impressed by his country's political system. So I put the question to him one day when we were strolling through the former legation area, now largely occupied by Russian commercial buildings: "Why are there no dogs in Peking?" The answer was prompt and straightforward: "There are no dogs in any of our cities. We killed them all." Nor was there any hesitation on the part of Mr. Yen when I asked him the obvious further question of why all the dogs had been killed. "They were all killed when the U.S. started germ warfare in Korea. We found the dogs were carriers of the germs so we had to destroy them. It was a difficult decision to make because we Chinese like dogs." Here at last, I thought, is what I've been looking for—a Chinese with a sense of humor. "Surely," I said to Mr. Yen, "you don't believe that there was any truth to the reports of germ warfare. You are too intelligent a person to swallow that propaganda." Mr. Yen, I quickly discovered, was quite serious. It was not propaganda, he assured me. He had seen the evidence with his own eyes. When pressed for details of the evidence, he seemed reluctant to pursue the subject and I abandoned the discussion so far as he was concerned.

At the first opportunity I tackled the Chinese Foreign Office for an explanation of the absence of dogs in the country's capital city. The target this time was Chen Wei, of the information department. A graduate of Harvard University, Mr. Chen was a smooth character who could, on occasions, be persuaded to drop the Communist mask behind which he hid a genuine American outlook on life. Much to my astonishment Mr. Chen's reply was substantially the same as that of Mr. Yen. He simply embellished the story by supplying the year and a few details. "It happened in 1952 when the U.S. aggressors spread germ warfare to northeast China," Mr. Chen volunteered. "There's a difference of opinion as to who was the aggressor in Korea," I reminded Mr. Chen. Ignoring this, Mr. Chen said that the dogs in northeast China had been the first to be infected in the germ warfare and that teams of executioners had been set up in every city to destroy all the dogs. "We had to do it to protect ourselves," he added.

Still reeling mentally from the realization of the effectiveness of Communist propaganda on some of the Chinese, I turned next to the Ministry of Health, thinking that here at least could be obtained an answer not infected by anti-foreign hysteria. I suppose I should by this time have known better. Mrs. Li Teh-Chuan, Minister of Health, gave this answer, presented here just as it came from the interpreter: "In 1952, to protect the country against the bacteriological warfare then being waged, a great nation-wide patriotic health movement was launched. The people everywhere destroyed dogs, rats, mosquitoes, and other pests, along with their breeding places. In factories, offices, and military units, everyone turned out periodically for thorough cleanups, and this is still being done." Since there seemed no use in laboring the point, I took the opportunity to seek an explanation of why so many Chinese wore white cotton masks, which gave the traffic police, street sweepers, and even young girls and boys the appearance of being fugitives from operating rooms. These, I was solemnly assured by Mrs. Li, were a carryover from the germ warfare period. They were worn now by all food handlers and by those doing dirty jobs and by any of the general citizenry who either had a cold or were fearful of catching one.

From then on I kept my eyes peeled for dogs but only in one city, Lanchow, in the northwest, did I detect any evidence of dog life. In the countryside could be seen a few dogs who had escaped the national dragnet and it always delighted and puzzled my interpreters when I drew attention to the presence of a dog. But it wasn't until I reached Shanghai that I heard what is probably the real reason why Red China's cities are dogless. I raised the subject with officials at the British Legation when I discovered a lively young terrier scampering over the compound lawns. The Communists, I was informed, permitted legations to have dogs, but they had to be kept on the property. They could not be taken out on the streets. One legation, it seems, had brought in two huge wolfhounds. The presence of the dogs was acknowledged by a terse note from the foreign office to the effect that no more dogs of that size were to be brought into the country. The reason? Really quite simple. Dogs, and especially big dogs, eat too much; and in a country that is chronically short of food, what could be a more practical solution than to get rid of them?

HERBAL MEDICINE

PEKING. For all its efforts to discredit the past (pre-1949, that is) China's government is willing to join forces with that past in the interests of expediency. China's Marxists are turning to traditional Chinese medicine as it was practised nearly 400 years ago, to compensate for the dearth of medical doctors. In China today, there are not more than 40,000 doctors trained in Western medicine, about one per 16,000 of the population as against an average in Ontario of one per 1,000. To fill the gap, the Communists have called into action about 500,000 herbal doctors.

There is every indication that the government plans to extend to these Chinese medicine men, who still treat headaches by sticking fine needles into their patients, the same position in society now occupied by doctors who have had the Western type of training. The Ministry of Health has established a special department of Chinese medicine and a national academy has been set up in Peking for research. The government has suggested to those trained in Western medicine that they unite and work with the doctors of Chinese medicine so that the traditional theory and experience may be systemized, put on a scientific basis, and made an integral part of modern medical science. As a result, many hospitals have opened departments of traditional medicine or have invited its practitioners to join their staffs as consultants. Perhaps only under Chinese Marxism is it possible to see doctors proficient in the use of modern antibiotics working side by side with men who work from a manual that dates back to 26 B.C. and a textbook that was first published in 1578. Now known as *Pen Tsao Kang Mu (Compendium of Materia Medica)* it has been recently translated into Latin, French, Russian, English, German, and Japanese, and lists 1,892 kinds of remedies and about 10,000 prescriptions.

The two main features of Chinese herbal medicine are acupuncture and moxibustion. Acupuncture is the insertion of metal needles into various spots on the body to stimulate and readjust the controlling and regulatory functions of the higher nervous system. Students practise on life-sized bronze models of the human body which have holes at the spots where the needles should be thrust in. The figures are then covered with wax and students learn the proper spots for treatment by sticking the needles through the wax. Moxibustion is the burning of a cone or stick of moxa (wormwood or any of the varieties of sagebrush) over a given spot of the body to produce a hot compress, so as to stimulate the nerves. The burning, it is said, does not hurt the skin.

The Chinese are crediting a treatment developed by medicine doctors more than 300 years ago with having made medical history by aiding the recovery of thirty-two children from an illness which, they say, has baffled modern medicine. The illness was encephalitis B, which occurs chiefly in children under fifteen and is caused by a virus which attacks the central nervous system. Traditionally the death rate has remained between 30 and 50 per cent. Those patients who do survive often suffer from impairment of hearing and speech, paralysis, and mental illness. Known to the ancient Chinese as summer pestilence, the disease reached epidemic proportions in Japan about thirty years ago and is still prevalent in China, although its incidence has been reduced by preventive measures such as inoculation with a special vaccine, and control of mosquitoes, which carry the disease. The Chinese claim the disease is not amenable to treatment with antibiotics such as penicillin, streptomycin and aureomycin, or to the sulfa drugs, plasma, and serum therapy. Only the Chinese method of treating it, they say, has proved effective.

The traditional treatment for encephalitis B was tried at a children's hospital in Peking by Dr. Chiang Chien-an, a physician of Chinese medicine for thirty years. Among the old-fashioned methods used by Dr. Chiang when he examined his thirty-four patients was to look at their tongues. One patient was Pao Chien-ping, the four-year-old daughter of a peddler. She had been given injections of sulfadiazine, headache pills, and other drugs by mouth. She had a temperature of 104.5 when Dr. Chiang examined her, and was not expected to live. First he removed an icebag from her forehead, maintaining that it would only reduce the fever temporarily. He also banned strong medicine designed to make the child sweat. This, he claimed, would be like squeezing oil out of husks. He ruled out the use of stimulants such as coramine, or sedatives for restlessness and convulsions, as being bad for an already upset nervous system. He changed a diet of milk, eggs, and other foods containing energy-producing proteins and fat to a thin rice porridge and fruit juice. A rich diet during fever, he said, would only be an added burden to a weakened digestive system and was like trying to put out a fire by adding fuel to it.

To counteract the poison and cleanse the fever from within, Dr. Chiang prescribed a variety of medicines dissolved or cooked in water. One ingredient he gave to all encephalitis B patients was gypsum, commonly used in China to lower fever. He mixed the gypsum in water with rice powder and other ingredients to make white tiger soup. The temperature of the patient dropped two degrees the first day and was normal by the third.

Thirty other drugs were used by Dr. Chiang. These included dried Chinese wild flowers, known as gold and silver flowers, husks of the wild shu tan flower buds, and mulberry leaves. These were for lowering the temperature. The roots of two wild herbs, yuan sheng and sheng ti, were used as energy producers. Medicines for calming the nervous system and treating comas and convulsion were made from the horns of the Siamese rhinoceros and the Tibetan antelope, from cow bezoar, musk, tortoise shell, and Baroos camphor from Borneo. Ginseng root was given to encourage natural resistance.

Toward the end of the six-day treatment, the little girl was given dried yuan sheng and peilan (a fragrant orchid) to cleanse the remaining poison.

In urging medical personnel to overcome any remnants of a contemptuous attitude toward old Chinese medicine, the Ministry of Health offered this advice: "To be skeptical is an attitude allowable and necessary in science. But this is entirely different from subjective denial of a true fact. When you are skeptical about something, you continue to study it and find the conclusion. That is the way in which science advances. Subjective denial which ignores facts is the arch-foe of science." In the spirit of this advice, the Academy of Chinese Medicine in Peking is testing the pharmaceutical properties of the many drugs used in the treatment of encephalitis B. The scientists are trying to learn which of the ingredients are effective in curing the disease and why. The tests, it is hoped, may also disclose new uses for the ingredients. Research is also continuing on the actual effect of the Chinese treatment on the virus, and on the final effects on the body when the disease is treated in this way.

FREELOADING FRIENDS

PEKING. The Chinese Communists are pathetically hungry for friends, so much so that they take the food out of their own people's mouths in order to entertain visitors. In their eagerness to prove to their countrymen that China's totalitarian regime is now accepted as being respectable by other nations, the Communists have created what Western newspapermen have dubbed "the freeloading circuit." Perhaps the Communist yearning for friends is best described in the words of an Australian correspondent who put it this way: "The Communists are unable to distinguish between the people who will be a help to them and those who have no influence in their own countries. The Communists have no selectivity." As a result, mainland China is infested with packs of fellow-travelers and pseudo-Communists, most of whom qualify for an all-expenses-paid tour of Red China merely by virtue of being unionists, adherents of some peace movement, or of being known in their own countries as having leftist sympathies. They swarm all over the new tourist hotels, monopolize the few buses and taxis available in the main cities, and gobble up the best foods.

Not all of the many thousands of outsiders who annually tour the mainland as guests of the Communists are there simply for the free ride. Some come in a genuine spirit of exploration and inquisitiveness, honestly seeking to assess Communism as an alternative to democracy. They have a substantial standing in their own countries. Unhappily, these legitimate visitors are lost in the ranks of the purely sightseeing guests who have been invited to China by the Communist government in the hope that they will drop a small crumb of favorable comment when they return to their home countries.

It was in Peking that I first encountered this new brand of Asian tourists, some of them minor diplomats and petty union officials, who have developed into a fine art the ability to travel in the countries within the Communist orbit at no expense to themselves. There were several hundred of these people quartered in the Chien Men Hotel, Peking's newest hostelry. That they cluttered up the lobby, the one elevator still operating regularly, and all the other facilities of the hotel, seemed to me at the beginning to be just one of those things. Since there was only one dining room operating in the hotel, it was often my fate to have to eat amid a succession of toasts, speeches, and songs from these visitors, who ranged themselves around long, linen-covered tables heaped high with the good things of life. They were inevitably accompanied by a Chinese Communist official, identified as such by the severity of his party uniform, cast in the fashion made popular by Chairman Mao Tse-tung. If the official was at all dismayed by the appetite of his guests for the wines, meats, and fruits that adorned the table, he concealed his reactions by the enthusiasm with which he responded to the many toasts to China's new order.

My curiosity about the status of these occupants of the hotel became more than an idle passing interest when I acquired a desire for some of the oranges that were whipped by me on their way to the festive tables. When I asked the waiter for an orange, he was sorry, but those he was carrying were for the big table. My attempts to buy an orange were met with the reply that there were none for sale. When I protested that there were platters piled high with them in the dining room, I was politely informed that "those are for our visiting guests." It did not take long for me to distinguish between my status and that of the orange-eaters. A careful check of the receipts for meals disclosed that they had consecutive numbers. I was the only paying guest of the more than 300 foreigners living at the hotel, and much the same condition prevailed at all the other hotels I lived in during the more than two months I was in Red China.

Perhaps I can best illustrate how little substance the Communists need to prompt them to roll out the red carpet for a foreigner by giving a brief account of a Canadian who contributes to a Toronto Communist weekly. He had just arrived in Peking from Russia where he had spent almost six months, much of it at a seaside resort for treatment of a stomach ailment. While in Peking he lived at one of its best hotels and made several trips to various parts of the country. I last saw him in Shanghai on his way back to Moscow to attend the youth festival there. The tab for the complete trip was being picked up by the Chinese Communists. They even supplied him with pocket money. The best they could hope for in return was a favorable report in an obscure party organ.

It is easy to identify the visitors whom the Communists view as being friendly. Their arrival and movements are carefully reported by the newspapers. The presence in Red China of paying guests like myself is studiously ignored by the Red press. It wasn't until I was leaving China, however, that the difference between myself and other visitors was clearly defined. While in conversation with a Chinese who is on the staff of his country's embassy in Pakistan, I asked him why there had been a delay of six months in granting me a visa in view of the fact that others have merely to express a desire to visit the country and they are immediately admitted. The answer was a long time forthcoming, but when it came, it was straight from the shoulder: "Why," my diplomatic companion asked, "should we put ourselves out for our enemies?" Here, then, was confirmation of what I had heard so many times in China—as a Western newspaperman I was automatically viewed by the Communists as an enemy and a spy.

The frequency with which I ran into groups of government guests quite naturally led to speculation as to how much they cost the government every year. I put the question to an official of the Foreign Office, who readily understood the "freeloading" appellation I attached to them. Still grinning as he contemplated this new addition to his vocabulary, the official pondered the question for a few moments. He did not, he replied, know how many of this type of visitor his country had. As to the cost, it really wasn't much. "Suppose," he said, "the cost of entertaining our friends means that every person in China gets one egg less a year. That's more than 600 million eggs. We can do a lot of entertaining at very little cost to our people."

172

ELECTIONS

PEKING. The constitution of Communist China, adopted in September, 1950, states that the country is a people's democratic state, led by the working class and based on an alliance between the working class and the peasants. The fact of the matter is, however, that Red China today is a Communist dictatorship, ruled by a hierarchy supported by a Communist party which claims to have the support of about 24 million dues-paying members. The Communist leaders freely and publicly admit that they govern China as dictators, but they attempt to soften the impact of that admission by explaining that the system is a people's democratic dictatorship. The obvious incongruity of linking democracy and dictatorship is blandly dismissed by the Communists with the explanation that the dictatorship is a dictatorship of the masses. In China, they say, all power belongs to the people, who exercise it through the National People's Congress and local people's congresses at all social levels. It is difficult for a foreigner who is accustomed to the Western version of democracy to reconcile the admitted intention of the Communists to strengthen the dictatorial aspect of their government with their claim that, under the constitution, Red China's citizens enjoy a wide measure of democracy and freedom.

In attempting to discover the extent to which the people of Communist China have a choice in who shall govern them, I discovered that to refer to the system as totalitarian touches a very sensitive nerve in the Communists. The many Communist officials through whom I explored the circuitous way in which the real government of China retains power instantly resented the suggestion that China has a totalitarian regime. I detected this reaction in others who were not yet party members but who hoped to be, and it was based, presumably, on the strictest definition of totalitarianism—a centralized form of government in which those in control grant neither recognition nor tolerance to parties of differing opinions. The Chinese Communists can legitimately claim that they are not totalitarian within the terms of that definition; the country's government is based on a united front of all parties, and the Communists simply have a preponderance of membership, holding all but a few minor posts. The fiction of non-totalitarianism is, of course, destroyed by the fact that the opinions of others are tolerated only so long as they do not suggest that a system other than Communism might be better for China. Those who express opposition to Communism find themselves publicly accused as counter-revolutionaries.

The change of government in Canada last June provided me with what I thought would be a clinching argument in the continual discussions I had with the Chinese on their political set-up. Armed with the results of the Canadian election, obtained via the British Broadcasting Corporation, I told one of the officials of the Chinese Foreign Office that here was proof of the basic difference between our system of government and that which rules China. "Tell me," I asked, "how you can change your government?" "But, we don't want to change our government," the official replied. "Let's suppose, for the sake of argument, you wanted to throw the Communists out," I said. "Just how would you go about it?" I truly felt sorry for him. He wrinkled his forehead and rubbed an eyebrow with a clenched fist. He squirmed and he pondered and then he terminated the discussion with this statement: "The electoral system of our country is such that it really serves to protect the democratic rights of the greatest number of people; it unites all forces that can be united for the cause of socialism; it is not a travesty of elections designed to defraud the people and protect the interests of the few." He made no apology for this direct quotation from party propaganda. Nor did he attempt to answer the question of how the Chinese could, if they so desired, change their government except through force.

The constitutional guarantee to all Chinese of the right to elect their representatives applies only at the lowest level of government. The basic electoral unit is a hsiang or town or district with a population not exceeding 2,000; it is entitled to fifteen or twenty deputies. If the population exceeds 2,000, twenty to thirty-five deputies are chosen. The deputies may be elected by secret ballot, but since they are invariably known to the people who do the electing, and since the number of candidates is always the same as the number to be elected, the choice is often made by a show of hands. From the county level up, all elections are indirect. Delegates to county people's congresses are selected by the district congresses from among their own members, and so on up the line to the National People's Congress, which is the central and all-important organ of state power. It is this body which chooses a chairman, who then appoints the premier, the vice-premiers, ministers, heads of commissions, and, in fact, the entire governmental establishment.

The electoral system of Red China can perhaps be illustrated by this brief report of what happened in Tsaikung-chuang, on the western outskirts of Peking. The nominations and elections were handled by municipal election experts sent from Peking; they prepared a list of eligible voters and selected a local election committee. When it came time for nominations, there was considerable discussion of what constituted ability to serve as a representative. Some said the important thing was to get around the hsiang and talk to everyone, so they suggested that a candidate must own a bicycle. Others insisted that education was a prerequisite. Still others said that a knowledge of farming was most important. After a long discussion a list of the necessary qualifications was drawn up: "The candidate must be politically dependable and a good worker, have a sense of justice and be loyal to the people. He or she must have a good personal attitude, and be capable of leadership in production." At a criticism meeting which all the candidates had to go through, one hopeful was asked, "Why do you always puff out your whiskers and pop your eyes? Why, if there are three ways of saying something, do you pick the most offensive one every time?" Admitting that he was honestly shocked by the criticism, the candidate replied, "I'm just like a tree; if it isn't pruned it'll grow wild. Your criticism is the pruning I need. It will help me to serve you." The election was held in a big, tree-shaded courtyard, festooned with red cloth streamers. A show of hands indicated that the voters agreed with the chosen list of candidates.

A newspaper report of the election commented that the voters of Tsaikungchuang felt they had carried out a very important task. More than ever they felt that the government and the whole country were their own. They were also happy that the electoral process had been so thorough. "Everyone chosen is fully qualified," said one woman. "We didn't satisfy ourselves with second-raters. We picked the best people in the hsiang."

MUSIC AND DANCING

PEKING. Elvis Presley and rock n' roll are aspects of the Western way of life that are beyond the ken of the people of Red China. Although I frequently and with painstaking efforts attempted to explain these phenomena to Chinese, young and old, they had been so well insulated from Western influences that I retired gracefully from the contest, always lamenting the inadequacy of the English language. The words required to convey the meaning of Elvis Presley, for instance, simply were not understood by the Chinese.

Had I been talking about the Singing Grannies of Shenyang we would have been on familiar ground. The group, officially known as the Shenyang Old Ladies' Choir, is frequently heard on Radio Peking, their thin and sometimes uncertain voices betraying their ages as they vocally promote the cause of Communism with such songs as "Granny Wang Demands Peace" and "The Liberty of Women." The choir was formed in 1952. None of its members is under fifty, and most are in their sixties. Their headquarters is a quiet Shenyang street and their conductor is a grandmother, Mrs. Tien Chun-yo, who is fifty-seven years old. In pre-1949 China women used to consider themselves old at forty or fifty. Old ladies of fifty or sixty singing in a choir would have been unusual, to say the least.

A few years ago, Mrs. Tien, called Granny Tien, found herself at a loose end when the culture and education department of the municipal government suggested she try to get the older women to form a choir which could give public performances on National Day, October 1 (the anniversary of the establishment of the Communist government), and during the Sino-Soviet friendship month of that year. It took a great deal of coaxing and cajoling on the part of Granny Tien before she was able to recruit a dozen members. Then another difficulty arose. None could read, let alone read music, and none could conduct or lead the singing. Granny's husband came to the rescue by agreeing to be a temporary conductor, and in the next few years the old ladies had themselves a time singing in factories, government offices, schools, army barracks, and other public places. Radio Shenyang recorded them and put them on the air, and the central newsreel and documentary film studio made a film about them. The singing grannies have acquired a repertoire of sixty songs and have given 300 performances to audiences totaling 300,000. When asked why old ladies should gad about the countryside singing, they reply with this song:

> Some folks think of us as poor old dears,
> Some folks say we're getting on in years,
> Wonder what it is makes us so hearty.
> Well, the answer to it's very plain,
> Takes but half a minute to explain;
> 'Cause we've got the Communists, our party.
> We sing of a China new and free,
> That her future's bright we all can see—
> Isn't that a cause for great elation?
> With the working class all in the van
> Life grows better with each five-year plan
> And Socialist industrialization.
> That's why all the old folks sing with joy,
> Men and women, every girl and boy,
> Textile worker, lumberjack and miner,
> Everybody's working heart and soul
> With his eyes fixed firmly on the goal,
> A very heaven on earth in People's China.

The teen-agers of Red China may not be familiar with the latest trends in Western culture as represented by rock 'n' roll, but the Communists have not succeeded in eliminating Western influence on dance music. Dances are comparatively rare, and those that are held are arranged by one of the many organizations established by the Communists to ensure that the Chinese follow the correct ideological path. Public dances as we know them in North America—dances for which the only qualification for admission is the price of a ticket—just do not exist. Nor is it possible for the general public to enjoy the luxury of dancing in the out of doors. I did run across one such night spot on the Sungari River, at Harbin, but it was not open to the public. It was the Riverside Club, operated by the local branch of the railway union. The requirement of being a railway worker was waived for me at the request of my interpreter. As a matter of fact, the unexpected and unusual appearance of a foreigner at the dance so confused and excited the officials that they neglected to collect the 20 fen (8 cents) admission from me. The dance floor was built on the bank of the river, and for those who wanted them there were boats available for rent. The pleasure of the Chinese couples who took advantage of the opportunity to be by themselves, floating in the reflection of the hundreds of multi-colored light bulbs that illuminated the dance floor, was marred to some degree by the inviting target they presented to those who leaned over the rail to clear their throats during intermission. Perhaps that was why the muffled creak of oars could be heard from mid-river, a refuge sought by some of the young couples as being out of range of their expectorating countrymen but still close enough to enjoy the music.

The music was strange, but not unpleasant. It was a rather agreeable mixture of Chinese and Western numbers. The fact that the Western numbers were enriched by the use of Chinese instruments probably explained the slow tempo in which the Chinese fox-trotted and waltzed to tunes which were on the hit parades of ten years ago. Frankly, I enjoyed this dance music more than the steady diet of Chinese opera and traditional music which tends to drive one to distraction, but my enjoyment was somewhat moderated by my puzzlement at the tendency of the Chinese young people to dance with members of the same sex. Fully three-quarters of the 200 people dancing were boys leading boys and girls leading girls. This affinity for members of the same sex shows up on the streets, where it is a common sight to see pairs of young men strolling along with their arms around each other.

For those not interested in dancing, or seeking a respite from it, beer was available at 22 fen (9 cents Canadian) a tankard, and it was in a discussion over one of these that I acquired a reasonable explanation of the seeming reluctance of Chinese boys and girls to dance with each other. Until just recently dancing in public had been frowned upon by the regime as frivolous and not in keeping with the march to Communism, with the result that Western-style dancing became almost a lost art. The pressure of organizations seeking entertainment as an outlet for the energies of their members has forced a relaxation of the ban to the extent that dances can be privately organized by authorized groups. "Our boys would much sooner dance with girls," Ling Yin, my twenty-five-year-old interpreter, explained, "but they feel so clumsy and awkward they hesitate to ask a girl for fear she would laugh at them."

COUNTER-REVOLUTIONARIES

PEKING. "We Chinese believe the true friend is a critical friend. When you report your impressions of the new China, I hope you will also criticize us." The speaker was Tien Chien, first secretary of the Chinese Legation in London. I could not help but recall his words when I saw the pained reaction of officials of China's Communist government to criticism of its handling of counter-revolutionaries. In its initial stages, this year's short-lived rectification campaign, launched by the Communists in May, appeared to be a mass application of the eagerness for criticism implied by Mr. Tien's advice. One criticism that resulted was the charge that more than 90 per cent of the cases against counter-revolutionaries had been mishandled. Premier Chou En-lai treated the charge as "sheer nonsense," but conceded that there may have been some errors in the practical application of the party's counter-revolutionary policy. That the accusation stung is shown by the fact that Chairman Mao has ordered a review of the handling of charges against those suspected of plotting against the regime. This task could prove to be monumental and perhaps impossible of achievement in view of the number of persons involved.

My efforts to obtain statistics as to the number of cases dealt with by China's courts since the 1949 revolution were fruitless. There was no resentment at my desire to ferret out the number of people who had been put to death in the course of what the Chinese Reds refer to as Socialist transformations —just a polite refusal to get down to actual figures. Among those who took refuge in the established Communist procedure—that of talking in terms of percentage changes—was Chang Chih-jang, vice-president of the Supreme People's Court. Since the subject of counter-revolutionary activity was one which the Communists themselves had made news with their claims that it was now almost non-existent, I naturally felt that perhaps the time was ripe for digging out some details of how the anti-counter-revolutionary campaign had been handled and the number of persons involved. There was a decided reluctance on the part of Mr. Chang to discuss the subject. He shied away from the direct question of how many counter-revolutionaries had been shot. He preferred to deal with criminal cases of all types, he informed me, adding that there had been a 50 per cent reduction in these during the past four years. "Fifty per cent of what?" I asked him. Mr. Chang looked away for a moment and then repeated his statement. "But Mr. Chang," I protested, "that's just like trying to say how high is up. It would be meaningless for me to report there has been a 50 per cent reduction in criminal cases unless I can also say 50 per cent of how much." While we were talking,

Mr. Chang was puffing on a tiny cigar, and he offered one to me as an example of the new cheap cigar now being produced in China. He pondered my remarks, all the while drawing heavily on the cigar, not much longer or thicker than a cigaret. Then he smiled and said: "My dear young man, I can't give you those figures. Not even our own newspapers have printed them."

The same double talk about percentages was engaged in by Premier Chou En-lai, but in breaking down the percentage totals he revealed enough to permit a reconstruction based on known figures. The result would indicate that at least 12 million Chinese have been charged with counter-revolutionary activities since the Communists seized power in 1949. According to Premier Chou, 16.8 per cent of the counter-revolutionaries were sentenced to death, because, he explained, "they had committed heinous crimes and public wrath was extremely strong against them." It is fairly well established now that more than 2 million were killed in the counter-revolutionary witch hunts. This figure was confirmed by Peking Radio. Again, using Chou En-lai's own percentages, 42.3 per cent were sentenced to reform through labor. Of these, 25.6 per cent have served their terms and have been released or placed in production jobs. There are, therefore, about 2 million Chinese still in custody and, in the words of Premier Chou, "being reformed through labor." Apparently about 4 million of those tried for counter-revolutionary activities were borderline cases. The only action taken was to deprive them of their rights as citizens and restrict their movements. All but about 400,000 of these people have been freed of surveillance. Premier Chou explained that another 400,000 were given clemency after arrest and were set free after some re-education. He gave no details of the process of re-education. On the basis of the Premier's own percentages it can be calculated there are now about 2 million forced laborers in Communist China. Here is their future as outlined by Premier Chou: "They will be given the opportunity to lead a new life if they atone for their crimes, abide by the law, and honestly go through the process of reform."

Perhaps a good deal of the difficulty I encountered in attempting to find out what was happening to these 2 million souls stemmed from the use of the expression "forced labor." When I referred to them as people being reformed through labor, there was a willingness to discuss in generalities the Communist justification for assuming that forcing a man to work would engender in him a love for and an understanding of Marxism. The Chinese Communist approach to slave labor has its basis in the principle laid down by Chairman Mao in his pamphlet on *People's Democratic Dictatorship*, now accepted as the Chinese Communist primer. Mao said: "As for those belonging to reactionary classes or groups, after their political power has been broken, we will permit them to make a living and to reform themselves through labor into new persons. If they do not want to work, the people's state will force them to do so." There is an understandable reluctance on the part of Chinese officials to pinpoint exactly where these slave laborers are being used, although it is admitted that they do exist. Hundreds of thousands are being used on various water conservation projects. At least 100,000 are at work in the Huai River valley where four big reservoirs have been built or are being constructed. About 10,000 are at work on the Friendship State Farm, one of the units in the Communist program to add to China's arable land. About 7,000 acres are being cultivated on this farm, which is in the north of China.

My first glimpse of slave labor at work was in Lanchow, in the northwest. We were feeling our way along a twisty gravel road in a 1957 maroon Mercedes-Benz, when we were passed by two trucks, crammed with men, their faces and hair tinted gray from the dust that hung over the road like patches of fog.

It was the presence of a soldier armed with a burp gun on the running board of each truck that quickened my interest. My guide was a member of the Bureau of Information and I knew him only as Mr. Wong. There was no hesitation in his reply to my query as to who were the occupants of the trucks. He said they were being reformed through labor and were being used in road work. Others, he said, were working on the new railway that was being built northwest into Sinkiang province. But the bulk of such people were working on the state farms. "There," he said, "they are making new lives for themselves. In time they will be joined by their families and will be able to have homes again—just as soon as they have cast off their old selves and taken on new selves." Here, too, was an explanation of the answer given by Tsao Hsiao Chi, an engineer of the reclamation planning bureau, when I asked him how he obtained his manpower. His reply: "By requisition from other areas."

DONKEYS IN DIAPERS

PEKING. Sometime later this year, probably in October, Communist China will have in operation an atomic reactor of the heavy water type, with an output of 7,000 kilowatts. The reactor, being built with the help of the Russians, is reported to be in the vicinity of Peking. Its power development is about a third as great as that of the reactor that is being built by Ontario Hydro. For all their excitement at this latest evidence that their scientists are, as Communist propaganda puts it, storming the fortress of science, the country's economists are more concerned with a phase of China's agriculture which is as old as the country itself. This is the collection of manure, both human and animal, which is organized to a degree incomprehensible to the foreigner. This organization is not to be entirely credited to the Communists; they have merely added mechanization to ensure that the country's millions of peasants can continue to crop the land as many as three times a year.

It is difficult to determine how much chemical fertilizer is being produced on mainland China because the Communists obscure production figures. It is a fact, however, that Communist China does not produce sufficient fertilizer, chemical or natural, to supply its overworked land, particularly now when the regime is attempting to stimulate the growth of wheat, which requires more fertilizer than rice. (The peasants are resisting this change in crops as much as possible but most of them are only work units in state co-operatives.) Communist China imports more than 2 million tons of chemical fertilizer annually, most of it from Australia, West Germany, Italy, and Belgium. This is not much. It is just about Canada's annual production of fertilizer materials. So, in view of the fact that China has a population more than forty times that of Canada, the importance of salvaging every scrap of natural fertilizer will be readily understood. Its importance was recognized by Premier Chou En-lai in his recent report to the People's Congress. He listed the collection of manure and the organization of co-operatives as the two projects that had received the main attention of the government during the previous year.

As part of the patriotic health campaign, the streets of China's cities, even those that are not paved, are frequently flushed by tank trucks similar to those that help to keep streets clean in North American cities. Sometimes this flushing is done twice daily in the hot weather to keep down the dust, but rarely is manure the target of the street washers, although most streets are clogged from sunup to sunset with pony- and donkey-drawn vehicles. The Chinese, ever a practical people, have combined thrift and the saving of labor by equipping their work animals with devices which might well be described as diapers, having in mind the service which the devices perform. As an integral part of its harness, every animal has a cloth bag strategically placed so as to ensure that the streets shall not be cluttered and that the droppings, so essential to the country's agricultural production, shall not be wastefully dispersed.

Mechanization has been introduced in the form of tank trucks, to gather the precious contents of privies and speed them to the countryside. A common early-morning sight on the streets of almost any Chinese city is that of Chinese children lugging heavily laden slop pails to be emptied into a long, dark-green tank truck left in the middle of the road. Chinese jog past it in the course of their daily business, unaffected by the stench. In some cities, where tank transport is not practicable due to a lack of vehicles, the night soil is delivered by the residents, generally the women, to central public latrines, which are then emptied into tank wagons. This widespread use of human manure for fertilizer is responsible for the stench which somehow seems to be an integral ingredient of the atmosphere wherever anything is being grown in China. Moreover, in this type of cultivation lurks a menace to the health of foreigners, whose constitutions have not had an opportunity to build up the natural immunity the Chinese possess. The dietary precautions which must be taken make for rather drab and dreary meals.

Ever conscious of medical instructions in Canada and England not to eat fresh fruits or vegetables unless I could peel and wash them myself, I had to sit unhappily and watch bowls of luscious strawberries, topped with whipped cream, being eagerly consumed by those whose hunger for such goodies outweighed their fear of being fertile soil for some oriental disease. The passing parade of strawberries and whipped cream was too much for one Czechoslovak woman who was my frequent dinner companion in a Peking hotel— she spoke English after a fashion and she saw in me an opportunity to increase her vocabulary. She had, she confided one evening, taken a dish of strawberries to her room in sheer desperation, and attempted to wash them. She had used hot water from the vacuum bottle (standard equipment in every hotel room) because not even the hot water out of the tap could be considered safe. The resulting mess was so unappetizing she had to curb her desire for strawberries.

It was my reluctance to gamble with my health that provided what was probably my most embarrassing moment in China. I was having dinner with an official of the Foreign Office. It was European-style food and a tempting bowl of salad—lettuce, celery, tomatoes, and cucumbers—graced the center of the table. We had almost completed the main course when my companion asked: "Do you not like salad?" When I replied that I did, very much, he wanted to know why I was not eating it. Without thinking, I blurted out: "It's too risky." I had only myself to blame for the necessary explanation, which became more painful by the minute. When I had concluded, my companion looked at me in silence. There was a suspicion of moisture in his eyes as he said: "Oh, you think our salads are dirty?" Although I frequently had to deal with him in future weeks, we never again recaptured the camaraderie I so clumsily destroyed that evening.

THE LAW COURTS

PEKING. "What kind of justice is available in the courts of Communist China?" The woman to whom I addressed the question hesitated momentarily as she sipped from a cup of green tea. Then she replied: "The days when the law was at the service of the rich and a burden on the poor are gone forever." There was no doubt about her sex, but the woman in question, Shih Liang, Red China's Minister of Justice, whom I judged to be about forty-five years old, had gone to great pains to sheathe herself in the austere clothing by which Communist officials outwardly emulate their chairman, Mao Tse-Tung. She was wearing loose-fitting men's clothes, and had drawn her hair straight back over her head in severe lines and tucked it in behind her ears. The sole bright spot in her costume was a multi-colored cotton jumper, a V-shaped portion of which relieved the flat monotony of her dark blue jacket. Mrs. Shih pursed her thin, almost colorless lips and added: "The Chinese have thrown off the yoke of imperialism, feudalism, and bureaucrat-capitalism and abolished all the privileges of the reactionaries. The working people are now masters in their own house."

It was nothing new to have Communist officials answer a direct question with an outpouring of propaganda. It came as a surprise in this instance because the interview had scarcely begun and because the speaker, so far as the record is concerned, was a non-Communist. Mrs. Shih is a vice-chairman of the China Democratic League, the largest of the so-called opposition parties in the united front government which ostensibly governs mainland China. She gave no hint, nor has there been any indication since, that she shared the views of two of her fellow vice-chairmen of the League in questioning the right of the Chinese Communists to rule mainland China. The two League members, Lo Lung-chi, Timber Minister, and Chang Po-chun, Communications Minister, together with Chang Nai-chi, Food Minister and vice-chairman of another opposition party (the Revolutionary Committee of the Kuomintang) have since publicly apologized for expressing what

188

the Communists describe as right-wing thoughts. There has been no word about their fate.

The question as to how people in Communist China go to law was prompted by the knowledge that when the Communists seized power in 1949, they scrapped the existing legal system. Legal justice since then has been administered largely by rule of thumb. "It is only when these regulations, decisions, and directives have proved effective that we can go ahead to sum up experience on which to draw up long-term laws," Mrs. Shih said. Red China still lacks a complete criminal code, civil code, and code of procedure. "As you can see," Mrs. Shih continued, "our laws are still far from perfect. Such a state of affairs must inevitably last a considerable while in a newly founded state. It is no easy thing to formulate all laws and regulations right away." She countered the suggestion that there is no law in Communist China with the claim that her country already has many of the new laws required. China has, she said, the National People's Congress, the people's courts, a trade union law, a marriage law, an agrarian reform law, regulations governing the punishment of counter-revolutionaries, regulations against corruption, and many other laws, decrees, and regulations governing the protection of labor, national regional autonomy, agricultural producers' co-operatives, and public and private joint enterprises. "All of these laws, decrees, and regulations, are, bit by bit, being worked out and perfected as we learn from experience gained during the people's revolution, experience acquired in running our country ourselves, in the light of prevailing conditions, political, economic, and social," Mrs. Shih said.

The chief component of the Communist judiciary is the so-called people's courts. These were organized in the early stages of the Communist regime to act quickly and compensate for the lack of lawyers. There are still only about 2,000 lawyers in

Red China. Regulations for legal practitioners are now being worked out on the basis of experience gained in this field so far. Judicial proceedings in the people's courts make use of a system of people's assessors. These—a sort of panel jury or lay judges—are elected. Any citizen, male or female, who has reached the age of twenty-three and has not been deprived of his or her political rights (as are counter-revolutionaries and former landlords) may be elected a people's assessor. The term of office is two years and election is generally by show of hands. There are about 246,500 of these assessors who are an integral part of a Communist court. Except for cases on appeal, which are heard by a court of three judges, all cases, civil and criminal, are heard by a court consisting of one judge and two people's assessors. The assessor has the same rights as a judge, an equal voice in deciding the judgment.

There are more than 2,700 people's courts in China, divided into four classes: the supreme people's court, which is the highest judicial organ and supervises the work of all local courts and specialized courts; the higher people's courts; the intermediate people's courts; and the primary people's courts. A primary people's court may, when necessary, set up one or more people's tribunals. These tribunals are a component part of the primary people's court and their judgments and orders count as decisions of the primary people's courts. The Communists made extensive use of the people's tribunals during the 1951 campaign against counter-revolutionaries and secret agents. On some occasions the tribunals consisted of thousands of people. Trials were held in open air, an oral verdict rendered, and the sentence, usually death, was carried out immediately, in the presence of the tribunal.

Another branch of the Communist system of justice is the mediation committee, which takes care of neighborhood affairs —generally disputes about rent, since a great deal of city housing is still privately owned and can be rented. In these committees is further evidence of the reluctance of the Chinese Communists to part entirely with their country's past, since it was a tradition of the Chinese empire that citizens should agree among themselves rather than seek judgment from a magistrate.

CAPTIVE AUDIENCE

PEKING. Perhaps the most vexing problem facing the Communists is how to get the party line across to a population 70 per cent of which is illiterate. Some progress has been made in the years since the 1949 revolution. In the seven years up to the end of 1956, it is claimed, 22 million persons were taught to read and write. On the basis of a figure given by Premier Chou En-lai about a month ago, this still leaves 455 million people who cannot read or write. This vast pool of ignorance is particularly irritating to the party's propagandists who are surely the busiest of all people in this huge country. China's presses have been running overtime turning out a tremendous volume of publications directed at a captive audience, the main bulk of which has to be content with having someone else do the reading for them. For most people in Communist China the only knowledge of what is happening in their own country and the outside world comes to them out of the mouths of party readers. These people are an integral part of community life and attendance at the daily reading of a newspaper or a government directive is as mandatory as reporting for work in the fields every morning at 6:00 A.M.

The 200 million-odd people who have the ability to look after their own reading requirements have a voracious appetite for the printed word. They read anything at any given opportunity. They walk along the streets reading; elevator operators can scarcely lay down a book or newspaper long enough to obey the angry buzzing of guests who have been kept waiting for several minutes. A glance in almost any doorway of a Chinese city reveals an identical picture—groups of Chinese, all young, huddled over some reading matter. For those unable to secure daily newspapers, hundreds of racks have been erected at the curbs of the main streets in the cities and all of them are greedily perused by Communist China's younger generation. Books are read and re-read until they are so dog-eared they would appear to be incapable of giving further pleasure, yet they pop up in used book stalls where a reader may, if he so desires, pay 2 fen (½-cent Canadian) and take the book home, or for half the price read the book at the stall.

For the most of these millions thirsty for knowledge, the Communists provide a rather thin fare, most of it designed to convince the Chinese that although their country's beginning was about 4,000 years ago, its history really began in 1949. The alternative for those who weary of reading that all that is good in mainland China today had its origin in 1949, co-incident with the seizure of power by the Communists, are publications which foster a virulent hatred of foreigners, of the United States (for its support of Chiang Kai-shek on Formosa) and of the Kuomintang, the government ousted by the Communists.

The most popular author in Communist China, if the number of books printed is evidence of popularity, is Chairman Mao Tse-tung. The sixty-three-year-old grandmotherish-looking boss of 653 million Chinese has joined the ranks of the best-sellers—10 million copies of the first, second, and third volumes of his selected works have been distributed since 1949. These selected works are, in the main, reports of lectures given by Mao as far back as 1927 and they cover subjects that are of importance in a Communist state, such as *Mao Tse-tung on the Question of Agricultural Co-operation* and *Mao Tse-tung on New Democracy*. It is to these selected works that the Communists turn for guidance when seeking an answer to the questions which inevitably arise in directing so many millions of people onto the path of totalitarianism. Another best-seller, in terms of volume, is *Son of the Working Class*. About 4 million copies of it were printed. Marxist-Leninist works also occupy a conspicuous place in Communist publishing activities. By the end of 1955, for instance, 226 works of Marx, Engels, Lenin, and Stalin had been issued to a total of 24,045,000 copies.

In addition to this vast outpouring of books dedicated to the dogmatic and dialectical education of the Chinese masses, there are 358 national and provincial newspapers and 465 magazines. The leading newspaper is *Jenminjihpao*, the *People's Daily*, published by the central committee of the Communist party in Peking. It is simultaneously published in other cities such as Shenyang (Mukden) by shipping mats to the outlying districts in single-engined aircraft made in Czechoslovakia. The *People's Daily* generally publishes an eight-page paper and sells for 10 fen (4 cents Canadian). Its circulation is reported to be 200,000 but it reaches many more readers through the organized newspaper reading-groups and the street racks.

Because the Chinese Communists reserve their valuable newspaper space for mention of those they consider to be their friends, the Chinese live in a lop-sided world so far as their reading fare is concerned. There is no dispute by the Communists that the world is round but a perusal of their newspapers would leave the impression that it contains only Red China, Russia, those nations which are under Communist domination and have recognized the Chinese regime, and those it thinks are likely to do so in the near future. North America and the other free countries of the world might just as well not exist so far as the reader is concerned.

One edition of the *People's Daily* which I had translated contained twelve pictures. Chairman Mao appeared in four of them. Here is a sampling of the newspaper's contents: a report of a garden party for Russia's Voroshilov, with group photograph; Mao greeting a Japanese trade delegate; a story on the double-decker bridge under construction over the Yangtze at Wuhan; Mao receiving the speaker of the Burma Parliament; Voroshilov visiting the Imperial Palace; a story on inner contradictions in the Communist party; a plug for the patriotic health campaign—on the subject of personal cleanliness; results of an economic survey in two provinces; almost a full page of drawings and maps of a dam being built at Sanmen; half a page of classified ads for opera and movies. An extra for the reader that day was a cartoon illustrating Uncle Sam pointing a gun at the Middle East with President Eisenhower crouching in the background. Not even my interpreter got the point of this, perhaps because it had taken him almost eight hours to translate the paper's contents for me.

In their emphasis on the party line that nothing good happened in China before 1949, the Communists go to great lengths to make their point. Sidewalks and buildings are clearly identified with the year of construction. After many weeks of being shown the evidence of what had taken place since the revolution, I finally said to an interpreter in Chungking: "Was there nothing built in China before 1949?" "Oh, yes," he replied, "but most of the buildings have been reconstructed." When I asked to be shown an example of this reconstruction, he directed my attention to the wartime head-quarters of the Chiang Kai-shek government. Unable to discern any evidence of reconstruction, I pressed him for details. He finally conceded that the reconstruction consisted of a fresh coat of paint on the outside of the building.

CHINA OVERVIEW

TORONTO. Since my return from Red China, the question asked most often has been: "How strong a hold do the Communists have on the country?"

Outwardly, at least, the Communists would seem to be in a stronger position than any of their predecessors. They have, for the first time in many decades, placed the huge, sprawling mass of mainland China under one central control. This control is maintained by an army now estimated to number close to 5 million. To this must be added a rapidly growing air force equipped with modern Russian fighter planes and bombers.

Behind this armed bulwark there are perhaps 12 million active Communist party members whose job it is to implement a Marxist blueprint devised by Mao Tse-tung, the sixty-three-year-old farmer's son who lives behind the walls of the Forbidden City, emerging infrequently to direct the course of Chinese Communism. The number of acknowledged party members may seem impressive at first glance, but there is every possibility that the party ranks have been fattened by an inflation induced by success. China's Communist party remained small in number from its founding in Paris in 1921 until it finally seized control of the country in 1949. In 1945 the party

195

strength was just over one million; its numbers had grown to about 5 million in 1951, so Chinese have been accepted into the party at the rate of more than one million annually since that year.

The Chinese always have been a practical people. They quickly adapt themselves to changed conditions and all through their long and troubled history they have demonstrated an unusual capacity for absorbing invaders. While it is true that Communism is not an invading force in the sense of having been imposed by people from without, there is no denying that it is alien to the Chinese nature. That they are not Communists by inclination has not, however, made some of the Chinese hesitate to seize the opportunity of bettering themselves when the occasion presented itself. It is conceded by experienced observers of the Chinese scene that many of the apparently enthusiastic party members are merely opportunists willing to align themselves with the proponents of an alien philosophy for the immediate reward of the slightly better standard of living which party members enjoy in Red China.

This is particularly true of the Chinese intellectuals. They have admittedly suffered greatly at the hands of the Communists since the 1949 revolution, but it was they, nevertheless, who founded the Communist party and it was they, rather than the peasants, who were the chief strength of the Communists. Without the leadership of the educated classes it is not likely the Communists could have fashioned the despair of the peasants into the weapon with which they eventually seized power.

As staunch believers in the doctrine that pleasure is the chief good, the intellectuals of China saw in the party an opportunity to continue their pursuit of the good things in life. They have had a rude awakening at the hands of the masters they served so well. They are now toeing the line of orthodox thinking, a condition brought about in most cases by a thorough ideological remolding conducted by Mao Tse-tung and his party chiefs.

The intellectuals are now a small minority in the party. They have been overwhelmed by a flood of young peasants and workers, attracted to the party ranks by the prospect of a better-than-average livelihood. That the Communist hierarchy suspects that the conversion of these newer members to Marxism is largely prompted by opportunism would seem to be confirmed by the recent rectification campaign. This was initially intended to purge the party ranks of members who were failing to emphasize their love for Communism by visibly demonstrating a high level of ideological understanding.

The rectification campaign unhappily got out of hand and in the runaway produced public criticism of the Communist party which must have come as something of a shock to Chairman Mao. Despite this sniping at the Communists, much of it quite vehement, there is little evidence at this time to support the hopes of the free world that Red China's government is weakening.

The Communists have a tight hold on the country. Cities are heavily garrisoned by troops whose loyalty to the regime is bolstered by regular pay, good food, and good living quarters. The peasants, the vast bulk of mainland China's population, are watched over by the party cadres who control small groups through the simple but effective method of manipulating food supplies. The effectiveness of this weapon on a people whose main concern in life is getting enough to eat is obvious.

II

"The plan will take care of it." That is a favorite retreat of China's Communists in the face of pertinent questions on the economic progress of the country. The Communists believe implicitly in the value of planning. They have a plan for birth control, a plan for increasing food production, a plan for this, and a plan for that.

Economic development according to plan is, of course, an import from Russia. The Chinese Reds, as is to be expected, draw freely on the experiences of the Soviet Union. In the light of Russia's failure to bring the living conditions of its people up to Western standards after forty years of totalitarian control, it is not surprising to find highly placed officials in China who are skeptical of the value to their country of learning from Russia. There is a substantial body of opinion in Red China which sincerely believes that the admitted mistakes and shortcomings of the Communists in China since 1949 are the result of attempting to follow in the footsteps of the Russians.

Naturally, the Chinese leaders consider this to be a harmful point of view. Yet their constant exhortations that it is necessary for China to learn from Russia are a tongue-in-cheek process, since these declarations of policy are frequently amended to the effect that the question lies in how the Chinese do the learning. "If we do not learn well, the responsibility lies wholly with us," the Reds explain. Then they further dilute the purity of their devotion to things Russian by saying, "It is exactly because we have conscientiously studied the pioneering experience of the Soviet Union that we have been able to avoid taking many unnecessary detours and so gained great achievements in our construction work. Of course, we should not mechanically copy the experience of other countries; even successful experience must be used with discretion, and in applying such experience care must be taken to see that it is adapted to the actual conditions in our own country." The speaker in this instance was Premier Chou En-lai, who added that it is not easy for the Communists to select the right kind of experience from other countries, and still harder to adapt such experience to actual conditions in China.

So it is that all that has taken place in China since 1953 has been done in the name of the first five-year plan for development of the national economy. All phases of development have been lumped under the one general heading, and whether the subject under discussion is birth control, education, or industrial expansion, everything is being done according to The Plan.

It is not an idle generalization to say that every facet of life in Red China is governed by The Plan. The Reds have brashly laid out on paper the increases which must be made in fields which scarcely lend themselves to predetermined increase. The Reds have not, so far as I could determine, presumed to dictate that so much rain shall have fallen by the end of 1957 when the first five-year plan is concluded. But they have quite blithely ventured into other equally intangible areas such as the living standards of the masses of people they control. The Plan demands that the material well-being of the peasants shall be improved. There shall be a 33 per cent rise in average money-wages for factory and office workers. At the same time prices shall continue to be kept stable.

Since, in the final analysis, it is the food supply which will likely determine the future of Communism in China, let us examine how it has fared under The Plan. China has seldom been able to feed herself. This chronic scarcity of food has been aggravated in recent years by the Communists who, in their haste to convert from an agricultural to an industrial economy, have robbed the country of essential foodstuffs. Recurring floods and an expanding population further complicate the problem. Last year's floods were not only the worst (despite The Plan) since the Communists seized power in 1949, but also the worst in the last few decades. This year's rainfall gives every indication of doing more crop damage than the 1956 downpour.

The compulsory participation of most of the country's food

growers in co-operatives and the establishment of huge state farms have not appreciably increased food production, at least not enough to adequately feed the more than 16 million babies born annually and to provide the increasing quantities exported by the Reds to pay for imports of industrial equipment.

An evaluation of the production figures is complicated by the tendency of the Communists to deal only in increases. They seldom use base figures on which these increases are determined, but a base is available in the case of agricultural production. In 1949 it was 32,600 million yuan ($13,040 million). By 1956 it had increased to 58,300 million yuan ($23,320 million). Comparisons are generally conceded to be odious, but what this production means to the average Chinese is perhaps more understandable in terms of Canadian values. The latest complete Canadian figures available are for 1954. In that year Canadian farmers sold their products for $2,377,834,000, or about one-tenth of the Chinese 1956 production. In China 520 million people live on farms, about 200 times the Canadian farm population of 2,800,000. This means then, that the average agricultural output per person on a Canadian farm was $850 annually, in Red China, about $45. There are no exact population figures available, but it is quite likely there were 440 million Chinese living on farms in 1949. Using the Communists' own figures of production for that year, production per person was increased by $15 in seven years.

The Communists themselves publicly admit that they are not impressed by their agricultural progress. "China," says Premier Chou, "is an agricultural country, a poor country, economically and culturally backward, with a large population. . . . our people's living standards are very low. The rate of improvement of living standards depends on the rate of development of production, and the rate of increase in the production of daily necessities and consumer goods . . . depends to a fairly great extent on the rate of increase of agricultural output."

The Chinese have one quality not always enjoyed by other people hitched to the Communist yoke. They are a patient, practical people first, and then Communists. Despite all the ballyhoo which surrounds The Plan, there is the sober realization, privately admitted by Communist officials, that their five-year plans—a new one commences next year—are but segments in the half-century it will take them to create in mainland China an economy equivalent to that enjoyed by Canada in 1957.

III

The Chinese Communists desire above all else to attain the high standards of living that prevail in the Western countries. Yet, in choosing the method by which to industrialize their country, they ignored the historical path which has made possible the prosperity of the West. The decision was made several years ago when the first five-year plan, which ends this year, was being blueprinted. The Chinese decided to turn their backs on the admitted success of the West in favor of the Russian way. Chairman Mao Tse-tung and his advisers, gambling that they could profit from Russia's experience, decided that they should lay first stress on the building of heavy industry. They ignored the possibility that this emphasis might conflict with the urgent need to raise their people's standards of living.

The choice made then by the Reds clearly indicated that the Communists in China, as in Russia, considered that guns should come before butter. Capital goods had to take precedence over consumers' goods so that China could manufacture the armament that an uneasy regime feels it requires to resist an attack by the democratic countries—an attack it considers to be inevitable. The country's rulers are still convinced that the free world has every intention of attempting to oust them by force, but the strain on an agricultural economy of the feverish race to arm is beginning to show. And the Communists are commencing to doubt the wisdom of having blindly followed in Russia's footsteps.

Perhaps the change of heart is best illustrated by the comment made to me in Peking by L. K. Yung, research director for the state planning commission. "Never again," Mr. Yung told me, "shall we indulge in the luxury of another Changchun." Mr. Yung was referring to the truck plant at Changchun (in what was formerly known as Manchuria), which was designed by the Russians and is designated by the Communists as the No. 1 Lorry Factory. I had just returned from a visit to it. There is not yet a No. 2 factory. The product of the Changchun factory is known as the Liberation Lorry. It is a six-cylinder truck, rated at 95 h.p., with dual wheels and a capacity of four tons. The vehicle itself weighs more than three tons and in appearance closely resembles a Dodge truck of about 1945 vintage.

The factory employs 18,000 people but was not operating the day I was there. It had, in fact, been idle for three days because it had exceeded its monthly quota as laid down by Peking. Some workers were taking stock or repairing machinery. Others were sitting around reading newspapers or magazines. The factory appeared to a layman to have been laid out in a modern assembly-line fashion. I had been told in Peking that the factory produced 30,000 units annually. The number on the last truck at the end of the assembly line was 3557. The factory manager told me that 3,550 vehicles had been turned out in the eleven months the plant had been in operation.

The factory, he explained, had not reached full capacity for several reasons. Most important was the inability of workers brought from the farms to absorb technical training. More energy was being expended in educating the peasants than in producing trucks. Production was also hampered by the failure of outside plants to maintain a steady flow of material not made at the truck plant. Then there was the arbitrary quota imposed by the government.

It was this restricted production that puzzled me most, but the explanation I received from Mr. Yung was reasonable in the light of my own observations in China. In a country desperately short of transport it was still cheaper to use man-power than to turn out more trucks. This became readily understandable when I inquired at Changchun as to the cost of producing a vehicle. I was told quite frankly that the cost was 20,000 yuan, that is, $8,000 a truck. Add to this the cost of gasoline at $1 a gallon, and motorized equipment becomes an expensive luxury. It was not the actual cost of production at Changchun that concerned the Communists. It was the fact that it represented a large outlay of capital tied up in an installation that was not immediately essential. Changchun is merely one example. The first five-year plan has produced many such instances.

There has now been a switch in emphasis. In the second five-year plan which ends in 1962 the proportion between the development of heavy and light industry has been adjusted in favor of the latter. The Reds have realized they cannot neglect the development of light industry which is still of major importance in providing consumers' goods. Light industrial undertakings, the Reds have belatedly learned, are relatively cheaper and easier to build. It takes no more than a year or two to put up a light industrial enterprise and in some cases after a year of operation its cost will have been returned. This is not the case with operations such as the truck factory at Changchun.

The Communists have also realized that light industry is one of their chief sources of capital accumulation, providing about 40 per cent of the state budget, since all profits go to the government. From 1952 to 1955 the profits made by the country's light industry provided the investment capital for heavy industry as well as its own and left a balance of 5,550 million yuan ($2,220 million) for other uses.

Prompting the decision to concentrate more on light industry was the ever-present fact of life in mainland China that it is still a predominantly agricultural country, with a large rural population. The Reds now realize that agriculture requires unflagging attention in their economic plans. Agriculture directly serves to feed and clothe the Chinese. It also provides nine-tenths of the raw materials for light industry. Two-thirds of the items China exports to pay for machinery that she cannot produce herself are agricultural products.

The entire economy of the country is still dependent on agriculture for prosperity. Here is an example of how a decrease in agricultural production affected the national economy. In 1952 there was a good harvest which resulted in a 32 per cent increase in the value of industrial production for 1953, adding an extra 12.5 per cent to state revenue. In 1954 there were widespread floods, industrial output dropped, and state revenue in 1955 increased by only 0.3 per cent over that of the previous year.

There was serious flooding in 1956 and again this year. The question now is whether the Communists have delayed too long their decision to reduce their bartering of the country's precious food supplies for heavy industrial equipment. That they may have done so is suggested by their recent plea to the Chinese to eat 25 per cent more vegetables, thus reducing the consumption of rice and wheat, which are so precious for trade and which have been the chief sufferers in the floods that have afflicted the country for three successive years. In reaching this decision to take what is, for them, a backward step, the Communists cannot be unmindful that it was the dreariness of a vegetable diet that prompted many Chinese to join forces with the Communists in the pre-1949 years and that eventually established them as the masters of the country.

IV

For most of mainland China's 653 million inhabitants, life is a dreary affair. There is little scope for fun-making in lives that must conform to the Communist dogma that labor is the most glorious thing in the country.

Yet, the very Communist rulers who have erased all outward evidence that the Chinese are intrinsically a fun-loving people permit themselves to be the public target of cartoonists and writers in a field where it is to be expected that Communists would be most sensitive to criticism—the quality of consumers' goods produced by a regime dedicated to the construction of a heavily industrialized base.

The Chinese are getting a lot of silent chuckles out of a cartoon which has had wide circulation on the mainland. That it was drawn by a Communist artist does not detract from its simple humor. It is a pen-and-ink illustration that depicts an undervest that has stretched so much in the wash that a grandfather and his grandson can both occupy the garment comfortably.

Other cartoonists have had their innings with two cats seesawing on a warped ruler; and with caramels so sticky that a dentist used them to extract teeth. Another drawing showed two children getting ready for bed; their father is sitting near by. The youngsters are contemplating their feet, which have turned red and green—the color of the socks they have just taken off. "Dad's feet must be blue," comments one child.

In Communist terminology, the production of shoddy goods constitutes a contradiction within the people. Contradictions, the Communists argue, can be corrected by criticism and self-criticism. All Chinese, they urge, must get into the habit of criticizing. The Communists believe themselves to be indivisible from the masses. Hence the strange spectacle of the regime actually encouraging widespread publicity of a decline in quality which had its origin in the elimination of competition —which resulted from the Communists' haste to socialize all the means of production.

China's Communist government is becoming increasingly aware of the basic economic fact that high-grade products can only be made out of high-grade materials. The regime has also had a costly lesson in the fallacy of depending on slogans and on fervor for Marxism to compensate for lack of materials in maintaining production. Last year, in an attempt to make less material go further, the Communists concocted the slogan, "Increase production and practise economy." Unhappily, human nature being what it is, the slogan was carried too far on occasion.

Some textile mills, anxious not to discard any spinnable fibres, turned out yarn and cloth that contained impurities. This is still being done. At a linen mill in Harbin, the manager apologized for the poor quality of the cloth. "It is the best we can make with what we have," he explained.

Another example of too enthusiastic an interpretation of the slogan was a powdered milk plant which began to pack its products in cardboard instead of glass jars. The result was that much of the powder became damp and caked in China's humid climate. "This, of course, was not really economy, but waste," the government quietly but firmly informed the guilty factory manager.

In pursuance of the belief that criticism should apply to all, the government organized an exhibit in Peking of what it dubbed "manufactured horrors." These included vacuum bottles (labeled Thermos by the Communists, in a fine disregard of trademarks) which had burst when boiling water was poured in; non-waterproof raincoats; rubber shoes with cracked soles; laundry soap that dried out to half its size during storage; matches that wouldn't light; fountain pens that either leaked or refused to flow.

The Communists called a special conference in Hunan province to inquire into the situation and it came as something of a shock to them to learn that despite their determination to learn by the experiences of others, the fault lay in an inherent weakness of totalitarian methods—the setting of monthly quotas for factories. The conference disclosed that many factory administrators thought only in terms of output, costs, and profits. One manager explained: "If we don't fulfill our plan, we are sure to be criticized. If quality is not up to the mark, that's not as serious."

Such attitudes were also fed by a Russian importation—the system of awards. A plant that completed its quota for volume and value of production, and for profits (all of which go to the state) was sure of a bonus. In 1955 a Hunan kitchenware factory got a bonus of more than 5,000 yuan ($2,000) even though its cooking pots were of uneven thickness and stayed on the shelves of the shops. This factory managed to make its planned profit only by selling some stock left from the previous year.

Out of this soul-searching has emerged a partial return to a competitive system—as competitive as it can possibly be under a system where the state controls everything. In restoring competition in a way which the Communists believe makes use of its advantages and avoids what the regime considers to be its disadvantages, all consumers' goods have been classified into two groups.

Basic products such as cotton yarn and cloth, sugar, paper, cigarets, and matches are still wholesaled entirely by the state. But each factory will be buying raw materials from the wholesale agency instead of receiving them, and will sell its finished goods to the agency instead of simply delivering them and being paid for work done. The quality is specified in the contract, and delivery can be refused if the goods are substandard.

In the second group are sundry consumers' goods for which a kind of free market relationship is gradually being set up between the manufacturers and the trade network (all government-controlled). State wholesalers have priority in buying, but any goods not sold to them can be disposed of direct to retailers. In addition, state wholesalers are forbidden to make compulsory allocation of such articles to retail shops (most of which are now run by the state). These shops are able to seek what their customers want from any source they please, going direct to the factories or to any part of the country.

To further the spirit of competition, the government has abandoned its system of uniform prices. It found that goods of different grades sold for the same amount in different places, so better brands tended to deteriorate. Now higher quality is to have its reward in higher prices.

V

"I'm past 50, but I've only really lived eight years." The speaker was Chen Wan-hsi, head of a sanitarium for dock workers in Shanghai. The sanitarium, a three-story red-brick building, was formerly the residence of the British manager of the Shanghai & Hongkew Wharf on the Whangpoo River. When the Communists seized power in China in 1949, Chen was forty-six. Ordinarily he would not be viewed as a malleable subject by the proponents of a philosophy which looks to the youth rather than the older people for its adherents. But Chen has been a Communist party member since 1954. In his way, perhaps, Chen is a tribute to the effectiveness of a propaganda line the central theme of which is that all that is good in China is a product of Communism.

The so-called Bamboo Curtain has rather effectively hidden from the free world the activities of the Communists in the largest unified land mass in Asia and the world's third largest country. While the outside world was guessing at what was happening behind the screen, the Communists were (and still are) methodically erecting a mental wall to block off any part of the pre-1949 history of their country which might still be viewed favorably by the Chinese.

Although their main efforts are directed at convincing the millions of Chinese under their control that 1949 was a turning point in modern Chinese history, Chairman Mao Tse-tung and the other party leaders are not adverse to scrambling aboard other band wagons if, in so doing, they can enhance their own description of themselves as the architects of a new China. So we find the Communists reaching back into China's past to link themselves with demonstrations of unrest by the population long before the teachings of Marx and Lenin were used to fashion a new way of life for the Chinese. The Communists are not above rewriting history to carve for themselves a leading role in industrial disputes which occurred long before the birth of their party in 1921.

Behind the propaganda front, Red China is still a land of grandeur and misery. It is a country where people who still use thread-like needles made of steel to treat headaches are being led by a militant minority along the path of Marxism, in transit in the dictatorship of the proletariat toward the ultimate goal of a classless state. There is a sparkle and a glitter about the new China, as it is being fashioned by the Communists, that is impressive. That this is as much a veneer as the false fronts of the main-street buildings that were typical of early settlements in Canada and the United States is not immediately apparent to the first-time visitor. The propaganda corps does its job well.

Yet it cannot be denied that much has been accomplished

by the Communists. Some of their achievements have been beneficial. They have stabilized the currency. Inflation still exists, but at a creeping pace. It is no longer necessary to have a basket of paper money to buy a meal. Nevertheless, the fear of inflation is still so uppermost in the thinking of the people that the regime has not yet ventured to circulate paper money with a value higher than 5 yuan ($2.50). Any higher denomination would be viewed with suspicion by the populace.

The Communists have removed corruption of officials by the simple but effective method of savage discipline, in some instances death. They have almost eliminated tipping. It is difficult to reward a waiter or a driver, because of an aversion to acceptance of gratuities fostered and maintained by lives so lacking in privacy that everyone knows exactly what the other person has in the way of worldly possessions. It would be difficult for a Chinese who accepted a tip to hide the fact from his neighbor.

There is the beginning of an efficient public-health service in China; new railways are being constructed and old ones rebuilt; a new industrial base is being constructed well inland, less vulnerable to military attack; a long-range program is under way to control the country's rivers.

Perhaps the greatest achievement of the Communists is that they have restored the self-respect of the Chinese. They have given them a national pride, an asset of some considerable worth in acquiring the support of even the most fearful anti-Communists.

It is unlikely that the free world will ever be able to fully measure the cost to the Chinese of these Communist achievements. Many millions have died that the Communists might have their way. For those who remain, life is poor at its best. It is not fair to compare living standards in China with those of the Western world, but by any standards the life of the Chinese in Communist China is incredibly poor.

The accomplishments of the Communists are all the more impressive because they have taken place in a country which has been in a tumult for half a century. And before that, the modernism of the outside world had been viewed with anxiety and resisted. Credit for all the new roads, new railway lines, new buildings, and, in fact, all construction that has taken place in China since 1949 is taken by the Communists. Yet who can say that what has taken place in the material sense in China since 1949 is due entirely to the efforts of the Communists? With or without them it seems reasonable to assume that some progress would have been made during the years since the revolution. No country, not even China, can stand still. And there is every possibility that just as much if not more would have been done for the Chinese by another form of government without recourse to the violent remolding of men's minds so essential to Communism.

Lightning Source UK Ltd.
Milton Keynes UK
UKHW010002210722
406167UK00001B/200